VALUABLE SELECTIONS FROM THE WRITINGS OF
FRANCES RIDLEY HAVERGAL

GRANTED
MINISTRIES
— PRESS —

HANNIBAL, MISSOURI
WWW.GRANTEDMINISTRIES.ORG

TABLE OF CONTENTS

PREFACE.

In a beautiful letter that Frances Ridley Havergal wrote to John Curwen, in which she described a work to teach Tonic Sol-fa music to teenaged girls and young women as a means to reach them with the gospel of Christ, she ended with these words: ". . . bringing them within hearing of loving and sympathizing words, and of the One name which is sweeter than any music." (This letter is found in *Letters by the Late Frances Ridley Havergal*, London: James Nisbet & Co, 1885, original book pages 68–69, page 165 of Volume IV of *The Complete Works of Frances Ridley Havergal*.)

In another statement posthumously quoted in the Prefatory Note to *Loyal Responses* with music (on page 1177 of Volume V of her *Complete Works*), her sister Maria V. G. Havergal quotes this statement by Frances concerning "Sacred Song": "I am delighted to have an opportunity of adding to the very meagre supply of Sacred Songs, and I hope they will be sufficiently tuneful and sufficiently easy for drawing-room singing. Some of those extant are very pathetic and dismal affairs! Why put off joyous singing till we reach the happier shore? Let us sing words which we feel and love, with clearness of enunciation, and looking up to meet His smile all the while we are singing. So shall we loyally sing for our King, yes for Him, Whose voice is our truest music."

Frances Ridley Havergal lived forty-two and a half years. She glowed the Lord Jesus Christ and His truth, and her life profoundly benefited many who knew her and many who later read her books or pamphlets or sang her hymns. Early in the 21st century, few recognize her name, and most of those who do only know of her as a hymn-writer. At the time of her death, she was very widely known and greatly valued on both sides of the Atlantic, and likely four million of her books were published between 1870 and 1900. There is true gold in her writings, help and enrichment to disciples.

She was born on December 14, 1836, the sixth and last child of Rev. William Henry and Jane Head Havergal. As a child she was called "little quicksilver," because of her liveliness and speed. Her mother's death, when Frances was 11, very deeply affected her. She fully surrendered her heart to Christ when she was 14, and though she had attended church and read the Bible for years, now she had the light and life of Christ she had not known before.

Though her formal education ended when Frances was 17 (concluding with one term at a girls' school in Dusseldorf, Germany, where she was awarded top prize, never previously done at the school), she was a true scholar and student the rest of her life. She was remarkably gifted (at or near the level of John Milton), and she was diligent with her gifts as few others have been. She was utterly fluent in German and French, and nearly fluent in Italian. Her tutor (a pastor in Switzerland) said that she read and understood the German divines and reformers with marvelous speed and perception, swallowing whole whatever he gave her to read (in German or Latin). Today few—almost none—realize the rare gifts she had in music, and the importance of her music. Frances' knowledge was only a means by which to know better her Saviour, and to glorify Him and to bring His truth and love to others. She read the original Hebrew and Greek texts, not as a dilettante but with real proficiency, diligence, and love. Her sister Maria wrote in *Memorials of Frances Ridley Havergal* and in *Lilies and Shamrocks* that she memorized all of the New Testament except the Book of Acts, all of the Minor Prophets, Isaiah, and all the Psalms. (Maria was accurate, would not have overstated any more than Frances, and sooner understated by leaving out details—books not completed, and various chapters memorized.) She loved the Word of God, and was intimately familiar with every page, searching and underlining and glowing till the end.

Much of her life was very crowded with so much to do: various ministries and projects, the care of her step-mother, and very important things to complete, and she was many times "put on the shelf" by severe illness or weakness and recovery. The love of Christ was her life, and she lived as she wrote, "ever, *only*, ALL for Thee." On June 3, 1879, she entered into His presence. Ten minutes before she died, she sang, faintly but clearly, the first verse of a hymn by Mary Jane Walker, set to music by Frances:

> Jesus, I will trust Thee, trust Thee with my soul;
> Guilty, lost, and helpless, Thou canst make me whole.
> There is none in heaven or on earth like Thee:
> Thou hast died for sinners—therefore, Lord, for me.

Her works are a gold-mine of help and enrichment. This collection of poems, prose pieces, and music scores by F.R.H. is taken from the edition of *The Complete Works of Frances Ridley Havergal*, now near completion for publication. The items given here are not better than other items in the edition, and a book twenty times this size could be filled with things as good as these: her other works are as fine and valuable as this small collection. This really is a very small collection next to all that she wrote; there is so much more by her, and the reader is recommended to proceed after this to whole books by her, which, if the Lord wills, we want to begin publishing soon. These selections are neither exceptional nor unusual in her body of work, but very representative: virtually all of her works are notably consistent—consistently rich—in the fineness of both the ideas and the presentation of the ideas.

There is life in these pages, and the reality of Jesus Christ. These pages truly glorify the Lord, and truly help, encourage, and enrich His people. There are also parts that are very powerful to reach those who do not yet know Him with the truth. "If the Lord wills," we desire soon to publish all of her *Complete Works*, and also many individual, smaller books taken from that edition.

David L. Chalkley

This book is published together with the new biography *"Ever, only, ALL for Thee" Frances Ridley Havergal: Glimpses of Her Life and Writings* by Pamela D. Bugden, a sterling biography based on the new edition of *The Complete Works of Frances Ridley Havergal*.

I. POEMS

LOVE FOR LOVE.

1 John 4:16.

Knowing that the God on high,
    With a tender Father's grace,
Waits to hear your faintest cry,
    Waits to show a Father's face,—
Stay and think!—oh, should not you
Love this gracious Father too?

Knowing Christ was crucified,
    Knowing that He loves you now
Just as much as when He died
    With the thorns upon His brow,—
Stay and think!—oh, should not you
Love this blessèd Saviour too?

Knowing that a Spirit strives
    With your weary, wandering heart,
Who can change the restless lives,
    Pure and perfect peace impart,—
Stay and think!—oh, should not you
Love this loving Spirit too?

NOTHING TO PAY.

Nothing to pay! Ah, nothing to pay!
Never a word of excuse to say!
Year after year thou hast filled the score,
Owing thy Lord still more and more.
    Hear the voice of Jesus say,
"Verily thou hast nothing to pay!
Ruined, lost art thou, and yet
I forgave thee all that debt."

Nothing to pay! the debt is so great;
What will you do with the awful weight?
How shall the way of escape be made?
Nothing to pay! yet it must be paid!
    Hear the voice of Jesus say,
"Verily thou hast nothing to pay!
All has been put to My account,
I have paid the full amount."

Nothing to pay; yes, nothing to pay!
Jesus has cleared all the debt away;
Blotted it out with His bleeding hand!
Free and forgiven and loved you stand.
　　Hear the voice of Jesus say,
"Verily thou hast nothing to pay!
Paid is the debt, and the debtor free!
Now I ask *thee,* lovest thou ME?"

EZEKIEL 33:10, ISAIAH 53:6.

"Therefore, O thou son of man, speak unto the house of Israel; Thus ye speak, saying, If our transgressions and our sins be upon us, and we pine away in them, how should we then live?"

"All we like sheep have gone astray; we have turned every one to his own way; and the Lord hath laid on Him the iniquity of us all."

ON Thee the Lord
　　My mighty sins hath laid;
And against Thee Jehovah's sword
　　Flashed forth its fiery blade.
The stroke of justice fell on Thee,

　　That it might never fall on me.

"BY THY CROSS AND PASSION."

"He hath given us rest by His sorrow, and life by His death."
—JOHN BUNYAN.

WHAT hast Thou done for me, O mighty Friend,
　　Who lovest to the end!
Reveal Thyself, that I may now behold
　　Thy love unknown, untold,
Bearing the curse, and made a curse for me,
That blessed and made a blessing I might be.

Oh, Thou wast crowned with thorns, that I might wear
　　A crown of glory fair;
"Exceeding sorrowful," that I might be
　　Exceeding glad in Thee;
"Rejected and despised," that I might stand
Accepted and complete on Thy right hand.

Wounded for my transgression, stricken sore,
　　That I might "sin no more";
Weak, that I might be always strong in Thee;
　　Bound, that I might be free;
Acquaint with grief, that I might only know
Fulness of joy in everlasting flow.

Thine was the chastisement, with no release,
   That mine might be the peace;
The bruising and the cruel stripes were Thine,
   That healing might be mine;
Thine was the sentence and the condemnation,
Mine the acquittal and the full salvation.

For Thee revilings, and a mocking throng,
   For me the angel-song;
For Thee the frown, the hiding of God's face,
   For me His smile of grace;
Sorrows of hell and bitterest death for Thee,
And heaven and everlasting life for me.

Thy cross and passion, and Thy precious death,
   While I have mortal breath,
Shall be my spring of love and work and praise,
   The life of all my days;
Till all this mystery of love supreme
Be solved in glory—glory's endless theme.

"I DID THIS FOR THEE! WHAT HAST THOU DONE FOR ME?"

(Motto placed under a picture of our Saviour in the
study of a german divine.)

I GAVE My life for thee,   Galatians 2:20
 My precious blood I shed,   1 Peter 1:19
That thou might'st ransomed be,   Ephesians 1:7
 And quickened from the dead.   Ephesians 2:1
I gave My life for thee;   Titus 2:14
What hast thou given for Me?   John 21:15–17

I spent long years for thee   1 Timothy 1:15
 In weariness and woe,   Isaiah 53:3
That an eternity   John 17:24
 Of joy thou mightest know.   John 16:22
I spent long years for thee;   John 1:10, 11
Hast thou spent *one* for Me?   1 Peter 4:2

My Father's home of light,   John 17:5
 My rainbow-circled throne,   Revelation 4:3
I left, for earthly night,   Philippians 2:7
 For wanderings sad and lone.   Matthew 8:20
I left it all for thee;   2 Corinthians 8:9
Hast thou left aught for Me?   Luke 10:29

I suffered much for thee,	Isaiah 53:5
More than thy tongue may tell,	Matthew 26:39
Of bitterest agony,	Luke 22:44
To rescue thee from hell.	Romans 5:9
I suffered much for thee;	1 Peter 2:21–24
What canst thou bear for Me?	Romans 8:17, 18
And I have brought to thee,	John 4:10, 14
Down from My home above,	John 3:13
Salvation full and free,	Revelation 21:6
My pardon and My love.	Acts 5:31
Great gifts I brought to thee;	Psalm 68:18
What hast thou brought to Me?	Romans 12:1
Oh, let thy life be given,	Romans 6:13
Thy years for Him be spent,	2 Corinthians 5:15
World-fetters all be riven,	Philippians 3:8
And joy with suffering blent;	1 Peter 4:13–16
I gave Myself for thee:	Ephesians 5:2
Give thou *thyself* to Me!	Proverbs 23:26

"NOW!"

A NIGHT of danger on the sea,
    Of sleeplessness and fear!
Wave after wave comes thundering
    Against the strong stone pier;
Each with a terrible recoil,
    And a grim and gathering might,
As blast on blast comes howling past,
Each wild gust wilder than the last,
    All through that awful night.

Well for the ships in the harbour now,
    Which came with the morning tide;
With unstrained cable and anchor sure,
    How quietly they ride!
Well for the barque that reached at eve,
    Though watched with breathless fear,
It was sheltered first ere the tempest burst,
    It is safe inside the pier!

But see! a faint and fatal light
    Out on the howling sea!
'Tis a vessel that seeks the harbour mouth,
    As in death-agony.
Though the strong stone arms are open wide,
    She has missed the only way;

'Tis all too late, for the storm drives fast,
The mighty waves have swept her past,
And against that sheltering pier shall cast
    Their wrecked and shattered prey.

Nearer and nearer the barque is borne,
    As over the deck they dash,
Where sailors five are clinging fast
To the sailless stump of the broken mast,
    Waiting the final crash.
Is it all too late? is there succour yet
    Those perishing men to reach?
Life is so near on the firm-built pier,
    That else must be death to each.

There are daring hearts and powerful arms,
    And swift and steady feet,
And they rush as down to a yawning grave,
In the strong recoil of the mightiest wave,
Treading that awful path to save,
    As they trod a homeward street.
Over the boulders and foam they rush
    Into the ghastly hollow;
They fling the rope to the heaving wreck,
The aim was sure, and it strikes the deck,
    As the shouts of quick hope follow.

Reached, but not saved! there is more to do,
    A trumpet note is heard;
And over the rage and over the roar
Of billowy thunders on the shore,
    Rings out the guiding word.
There is one chance, and only one,
    All can be saved, but how?
"The rope hold fast, but quit the mast
    At the trumpet-signal 'NOW!'"

There is a moment when the sea
    Has spent its furious strength;
A shuddering pause with a sudden swirl,
Gathering force again to hurl
Billow on billow in whirl on whirl;
    That moment comes at length—
With a single shout the *"Now"* peals out,
    And the answering leap is made.
Well for the simple hearts that just
Loosing the mast with fearless trust,
    The strange command obeyed!

For the rope is good, and the stout arms pull
 Ere the brief storm-lull is o'er;
It is but a swift and blinding sweep
Through the waters wild and dark and deep,
 And the men are safe on shore—
Safe! though the fiend-like blast pursue,
 Safe! though the waves dash high;
But the ringing cheer that rises clear
 Is pierced with a sudden cry:

"There are but four drawn up to shore,
 And five were on the deck!"
And the straining gaze that conquers gloom
Still traces, drifting on to doom,
 One man upon the wreck.
Again they chase in sternest race
 The far-recoiling wave;
The rope is thrown to the tossing mark,
But reaches not in the windy dark
 The one they strive to save.

Again they rush, and again they fail,
 Again, and yet again:
The storm yells back defiance loud,
The breakers rear a rampart proud,
 And roar, "In vain, in vain!"

Then a giant wave caught up the wreck,
 And bore it on its crest;
One moment it hung quivering there
 In horrible arrest.
And the lonely man on the savage sea
 A lightning flash uplit,
Still clinging fast to the broken mast
 That he had not dared to quit.

Then horror of great darkness fell,
 While eyes flashed inward fire;
And over all the roar and dash,
Through that great blackness came a crash,
 A token sure and dire.
The wave had burst upon the pier,
 The wreck was scattered wide;
Another *"Now"* would never reach
The corpse that lay upon the beach
 With the receding tide.

God's *"Now"* is sounding in your ears;
    Oh, let it reach your heart!
Not only from your sinfulness
    He bids you part;
Your righteousness as filthy rags
    Must all relinquished be,
And only Jesus' precious death
    Must be your plea.

Now trust the one provided rope,
    Now quit the broken mast,
Before the hope of safety be
    For ever past.
Fear not to trust His simple word,
    So sweet, so tried, so true,
And you are safe for evermore;
    Yes,—even you!

"And the Spirit and the bride say, Come. And let him that heareth say, Come. And let him that is athirst come. And whosoever will, let him take the water of life freely." —Revelation 22:17.

"Come unto me, all ye that labour and are heavy laden, and I will give you rest. Take my yoke upon you, and learn of me; for I am meek and lowly in heart: and ye shall find rest unto your souls. For my yoke is easy, and my burden is light." —Matthew 11:28-30.

WITHOUT CHRIST.

"At that time ye were without Christ."—Ephesians 2:12.

I COULD not do without Thee,	John 6:68
O Saviour of the lost!	Luke 19:10
Whose precious blood redeemed me,	1 Peter 1:18, 19
At such tremendous cost.	Revelation 5:9
Thy righteousness, Thy pardon,	Romans 3:22
Thy precious blood—must be	Ephesians 1:7
My only hope and comfort,	Hebrews 6:19
My glory and my plea.	Galatians 6:14
I could not do without Him!	Psalm 73:23
Jesus is more to me	Song. 5:10
Than all the richest, fairest gifts	Philippians 3:8
Of earth could ever be.	Matthew 13:44
But the more I find Him precious,	1 Peter 2:7
And the more I find Him true,	Psalm 18:2
The more I long for you to find	Psalm 34:8
What He can be to you.	John 1:46

You need not do without Him,
　For He is passing by;
He is waiting to be gracious,
　Only waiting for your cry.
He is waiting to receive you,—
　To make you all His own!
Why will you do without Him,
　And wander on alone?

Why will you do without Him?
　Is He not kind indeed?
Did He not die to save you?
　Is He not all you need?
Do you not want a Saviour?
　Do you not want a Friend?
One who will love you faithfully,
　And love you to the end?

Why will you do without Him?
　The Word of God is true;
The world is passing to its doom,
　And you are passing too.
It may be, no to-morrow
　Shall dawn for you or me;
Why will you run the awful risk
　Of all eternity?

What will you do without Him
　In the long and dreary day
Of trouble and perplexity,
　When you do not know the way;
And no one else can help you,
　And no one guides you right,
And hope comes not with morning,
　And rest comes not with night?

You could not do without Him,
　If once He made you see
The fetters that enchain you
　Till He hath set you free;
If once you saw the fearful load
　Of sin upon your soul,—
The hidden plague that ends in death,
　Unless He makes you whole!

Hosea 13:9
Matthew 20:30
Isaiah 30:18
Isaiah 30:19
2 Cor. 6:17
Isaiah 43:1
Hosea 11:8
Hosea 14:2

Hosea 13:10
Titus 3:4
Romans 5:8
John 4:14
Acts 5:31
John 15:14
Hosea 2:20
John 13:1

Jeremiah 4:30
Matthew 24:35
1 John 2:17
Psalm 144:4
James 4:14
Proverbs 27:1
Proverbs 29:1
Isaiah 33:14

Hosea 9:5
Eccles. 12:1
Isaiah 59:9, 10
Hosea 2:6
Hosea 13:9, 10
Jeremiah 2:17
Jeremiah 2:25
Job 7:4

Romans 7:24
John 8:33, 34
2 Peter 2:19
Romans 8:2
Psalm 38:4
Ezekiel 33:10
Jeremiah 17:9
Jeremiah 17:14

What will you do without Him	Jeremiah 12:5
When death is drawing near,	Eccles. 12:3
Without His love—the only love	Song. 8:6, 7
That casts out every fear;	1 John 4:18
When the shadow-valley opens,	Jeremiah 13:16
Unlighted and unknown,	Job 8:13, 14
And the terrors of its darkness	Job 10:21, 22
Must all be passed alone?	Psalm 23:4
What will you do without Him	Revelation 6:17
When the great White Throne is set,	Revelation 20:11
And the Judge who never can mistake,	Romans 2:16
And never can forget,—	Hosea 7:2
The Judge, whom you have never here	2 Cor. 5:10
As Friend and Saviour sought,	Matthew 7:23
Shall summon you to give account	Romans 14:12
Of deed, and word, and thought?	Matthew 12:36
What will you do without Him	Matthew 25:11
When He hath shut the door,	Revelation 3:7
And you are left outside, because	Hebrews 3:19
You would not come before;	John 5:40
When it is no use knocking,	Luke 13:25
No use to stand and wait,	Hebrews 12:17
For the word of doom tolls through your heart,	Revelation 22:11
That terrible "Too late"?	Luke 16:26
You cannot do without Him!	John 14:6
There is no other name	1 Timothy 2:5
By which you ever *can* be saved,—	Acts 4:12
No way, no hope, no claim!	Ephesians 2:12
Without Him—everlasting loss	Mark 8:36
Of love, and life, and light!	John 3:36
Without Him—everlasting woe,	Matthew 25:41
And everlasting night.	Matthew 8:12
But with Him—oh! *with Jesus!*—	Song. 4:8
Are any words so blest?	John 17:24
With Jesus—everlasting joy	Isaiah 35:10
And everlasting rest!	1 Thess. 4:17
With Jesus—all the empty heart	Psalm 107:9
Filled with His perfect love!	Ephesians 3:19, 20
With Jesus—perfect peace below,	Isaiah 26:3
And perfect bliss above!	Psalm 16:11

Why should you do without Him?—	Jeremiah 5:31
It is not yet too late;	Revelation 3:20
He has not closed the day of grace,	2 Cor. 6:2
He has not shut the gate.	Matthew 7:13
He calls you!—hush!	Mark 10:49
He calls you!—He would not have you go	John 6:67
Another step without Him,	Hosea 2:14
Because He loves you so.	John 15:13

Why will you do without Him?	Ezekiel 33:11
He calls and calls again—	John 7:37
"Come unto Me! Come unto Me!"	Matthew 11:28
Oh, shall He call in vain?	Isaiah 65:1, 2
He wants to have you with Him;	Matthew 23:37
Do you not want Him too?	Psalm 13:1, 2
You cannot do without Him,	1 John 5:12
And He wants—even you!	Jeremiah 31:3

WILL YOU NOT COME?

"Thou hast received gifts for men; yea, for the rebellious also."
—PSALM 68:18.

WILL you not come to Him for life?	John 5:40
Why will ye die, oh why?	Ezekiel 33:11
He gave His life for you, for you!	John 10:11
The gift is free, the word is true!	Romans 6:23
Will you not come? oh, why will you die?	2 Cor. 5:20

Will you not come to Him for peace—	Acts 10:36
Peace through His cross alone?	Colossians 1:20
He shed His precious blood for you;	1 Peter 1:19
The gift is free, the word is true!	Romans 5:15, 18
He is our Peace! oh, is He your own?	Ephesians 2:14

Will you not come to Him for rest?	Jeremiah 6:16
All that are weary, come!	Matthew 11:28
The rest He gives is deep and true;	Isaiah 11:10
'Tis offered now, 'tis offered you!	Isaiah 28:12
Rest in His love, and rest in His home.	Hebrews 4:3, 9

Will you not come to Him for joy,—	Matthew 13:44
Will you not come for this?	John 16:24
He laid His joys aside for you,	Philippians 2:7, 8
To give you joy, so sweet, so true!	John 15:11
Sorrowing heart, oh, drink of the bliss!	Romans 15:13

Will you not come to Him for love—	Ephesians 3:19
Love that can fill the heart,	Psalm 107:9
Exceeding great, exceeding free?	Ephesians 2:4
He loveth you, He loveth me!	Revelation 1:5
Will you not come? Why stand you apart?	Romans 5:8
Will you not come to Him for *all?*	John 4:14
Will you not "taste and see"?	Psalm 34:8
He waits to give it all to you;	Isaiah 30:18
The gifts are free, the words are true!	Matthew 7:7, 8
Jesus is calling, "Come unto Me!"	John 7:37

TO THEE.

"Lord, to whom shall we go?"—JOHN 6:68.

I BRING my sins to Thee,
   The sins I cannot count,
That all may cleansèd be
   In Thy once opened Fount.
I bring them, Saviour, all to Thee,
The burden is too great for me.

My heart to Thee I bring,
   The heart I cannot read;
A faithless, wandering thing,
   An evil heart indeed.
I bring it, Saviour, now to Thee,
That fixed and faithful it may be.

To Thee I bring my care,
   The care I cannot flee;
Thou wilt not only share,
   But bear it all for me.
O loving Saviour, now to Thee
I bring the load that wearies me.

I bring my grief to Thee,
   The grief I cannot tell;
No words shall needed be,
   Thou knowest all so well.
I bring the sorrow laid on me,
O suffering Saviour, now to Thee.

My joys to Thee I bring,
   The joys Thy love hath given,
That each may be a wing
   To lift me nearer heaven.
I bring them, Saviour, all to Thee,
For Thou hast purchased all for me.

My life I bring to Thee,
   I would not be my own;
O Saviour, let me be
   Thine ever, Thine alone.
My heart, my life, my all I bring
To Thee, my Saviour and my King!

DESPISED, REJECTED, WOUNDED NOW.

DESPISED, rejected, wounded now,
   Bowed 'neath a cross of shame,
With visage marred, with bleeding brow,
   Know ye the sufferer's name?

O Man of Sorrows!—Is this He
   Who human form should wear,
And with transgressors numbered be,
   Our mighty sins to bear?

O Son of God, who unto death
Hast loved, so lovèd me,
Henceforth be all my life and breath
Devoted unto Thee.

THE OPENED FOUNTAIN.

"A fountain opened for sin and for uncleanliness . . . Wounded in the
house of My friends."—ZECHARIAH 13:1, 6.

AND I have wounded Thee—oh, wounded Thee!—
Wounded the dear, dear Hand that holds me fast!
Oh, to recall the word! That cannot be!
Oh, to unthink the thought that out of reach hath passed!

Sorrow and bitter grief replace my bliss;
I could not wish that any joy should be;
There is no room for any thought but this,
That I have sinned—have sinned—have wounded Thee!

How *could* I grieve Thee so! Thou couldst have kept;
My fall was not the failure of Thy word.
Thy promise hath no flaw, no dire "except,"
To neutralize the grace so royally conferred.

Oh the exceeding sinfulness of sin!
Tenfold exceeding in the love-lit light
Of Thy sufficient grace, without, within,
Enough for every need, in never-conquered might!

With all the shame, with all the keen distress,
Quick, "waiting not," I flee to Thee again;
Close to the wound, belovèd Lord, I press,
That Thine own precious blood may overflow the stain.

O *precious* blood! Lord, let it rest on me!
I ask not only pardon from my King,
But cleansing from my Priest. I come to Thee
Just as I came at first,—a sinful, helpless thing.

Oh, cleanse me now! My Lord, I cannot stay
For evening shadows and a silent hour:
Now I have sinned, and *now*, with no delay,
I claim Thy promise and its total power.

O Saviour, bid me "go and sin no more,"
And keep me always "neath the mighty flow
Of Thy perpetual fountain; I implore
That Thy perpetual cleansing I may fully know.

THE PRECIOUS BLOOD OF JESUS.

PRECIOUS, precious blood of Jesus,
 Shed on Calvary;
Shed for rebels, shed for sinners,
 Shed for me.

Precious blood, that hath redeemed us!
 All the price is paid;
Perfect pardon now is offered,
 Peace is made.

Precious, precious blood of Jesus,
 Let it make thee whole;
Let it flow in mighty cleansing
 O'er thy soul.

Though thy sins are red like crimson,
 Deep in scarlet glow,
Jesu's precious blood can make them
 White as snow.

Now the holiest with boldness
 We may enter in,
For the open fountain cleanseth
 From all sin.

Precious blood! by this we conquer
 In the fiercest fight,
Sin and Satan overcoming
 By its might.

Precious, precious blood of Jesus,
 Ever flowing free!
O believe it, O receive it,
 'Tis for thee!

Precious blood, whose full atonement
 Makes us nigh to God!
Precious blood, our song of glory,
 Praise and laud!

LEANING OVER THE WATERFALL.

A young lady, aged 20, fell over the rocks at the Swallow Waterfall in the summer of 1873, and was lost to sight in a moment. The body was not recovered till four hours afterwards.

Leaning over the waterfall!
   Lured by the fairy sight,
Heeding not the warning call,
   Watching the foam and the flow,
Smooth and dark, or swift and bright,
Here in the shade and there in the light!
      Oh, who could know
The coming sorrow, the nearing woe!

Leaning over the waterfall!
   Only a day before
She had spoken of Jesu's wondrous call,
   As He trod the waves of Galilee.
They asked, as she gazed from the sunset shore,
" If He walked that water, what would you do ? "
Then fell the answer, glad and true,
     " If He beckoned me,
I would go to Him on the pathless sea."

Leaning over the waterfall
   Only a moment before!
And then the slip, the helpless call,
   The plunge unheard in the pauseless roar
   By the startled watchers on the shore;
And the feet that stood by the waterfall,
     So fair and free,
Are standing with Christ by the crystal sea.

Leaning over the waterfall!
   Have you not often leant
(What should hinder? or what appall?)
Freely, fearlessly, over the brink,
   Merrily glancing adown the stream,
   Or gazing wrapt in a musical dream
At the lovely waters? But pause and think—
     Who kept *your* feet,
And suffered you not such death to meet?

Leaning over the waterfall!
   What if *your* feet had slipped?
Never a moment of power to call,
   Never a hand in time to save
   From the terrible rush of the ruthless wave!
Hearken! would it be ill or well
     If thus *you* fell?
Hearken! would it be heaven or hell?

Leaning over the waterfall!
   Listen, and learn, and lean!
Listen to Him whose loving call
   Soundeth deep in your heart to-day!
   Learn of Jesus, the only way,
How to be holy, how to be blest!
     Lean on His breast,
And yours shall be safety and joy and rest.

BEHOLD YOUR KING.

"Behold, and see if there be any sorrow like unto My sorrow."
—LAMENTATIONS 1:12.

BEHOLD your King! Though the moonlight steals
   Through the silvery sprays of the olive tree,
No star-gemmed sceptre or crown it reveals,
   In the solemn shade of Gethsemane.
     Only a form of prostrate grief,
     Fallen, crushed, like a broken leaf!
Oh, think of His sorrow! that we may know
The depth of love in the depth of woe.

Behold your King! Is it nothing to you,
   That the crimson tokens of agony
From the kingly brow must fall like dew,
   Through the shuddering shades of Gethsemane?
     Jesus Himself, the Prince of Life,
     Bows in mysterious mortal strife;
Oh, think of His sorrow! that we may know
The unknown love in the unknown woe.

Behold your King, with His sorrow crowned,
   Alone, alone in the valley is He!
The shadows of death are gathering round,
   And the Cross must follow Gethsemane.
     Darker and darker the gloom must fall,
     Filled is the Cup, He must drink it all!
Oh, think of His sorrow! that we may know
His wondrous love in His wondrous woe.

AN EASTER PRAYER.

   OH let me know
The power of Thy resurrection;
   Oh let me show
Thy risen life in calm and clear reflection;
   Oh let me soar

Where Thou, my Saviour Christ, art gone before;
 In mind and heart
Let me dwell always, only, where Thou art.

 Oh let me give
Out of the gifts Thou freely givest;
 Oh let me live
With life abundantly because Thou livest;
 Oh make me shine
In darkest places, for Thy light is mine;
 Oh let me be
A faithful witness for Thy truth and Thee.

 Oh let me show
The strong reality of gospel story;
 Oh let me go
From strength to strength, from glory unto glory,
 Oh let me sing
For very joy, because Thou art my King;
 Oh let me praise
Thy love and faithfulness through all my days.

WHAT THOU WILT.

Do what Thou wilt! Yes, only do
 What seemeth good to Thee:
Thou art so loving, wise, and true,
 It must be best for me.

Send what Thou wilt; or beating shower,
 Soft dew, or brilliant sun;
Alike in still or stormy hour,
 My Lord, Thy will be done.

Teach what Thou wilt; and make me learn
 Each lesson full and sweet,
And deeper things of God discern
 While sitting at Thy feet.

Say what Thou wilt; and let each word
 My quick obedience win;
Let loyalty and love be stirred
 To deeper glow within.

Give what Thou wilt; for then I know
 I shall be rich indeed;
My King rejoices to bestow
 Supply for every need.

Take what Thou wilt, belovèd Lord,
   For I have all in Thee!
My own exceeding great reward,
   Thou, Thou Thyself shalt be!

KNOWING.

I KNOW the crimson stain of sin,
Defiling all without, within;
But now rejoicingly I know
That He has washed me white as snow.
I praise Him for the cleansing tide,
Because I know that Jesus died.

I know the helpless, hopeless plaint,
"The whole head sick, the whole heart faint";
But now I trust His touch of grace,
That meets so perfectly my case,
So tenderly, so truly deals;
Because I know that Jesus heals.

I know the pang of forfeit breath,
When life in sin was life in death;
But now I know His life is mine,
And nothing shall that cord untwine,
Rejoicing in the life He gives,
Because I know that Jesus lives.

I know how anxious thought can press,
I know the weight of carefulness;
But now I know the sweet reward
Of casting all upon my Lord,
No longer bearing what He bears,
Because I know that Jesus cares.

I know the sorrow that is known
To the tear-burdened heart alone;
But now I know its full relief
Through Him who was acquaint with grief,
And peace through every trial flows,
Because I know that Jesus knows.

I know the gloom amid the mirth,
The longing for the love of earth;
But now I know the Love that fills,
That gladdens, blesses, crowns, and stills,
That nothing mars and nothing moves,—
I know, I know that Jesus loves.

I know the shrinking and the fear,
When all seems wrong, and nothing clear;
But now I gaze upon His throne,
And faith sees all His foes o'erthrown,
And I can wait till He explains,
Because I know that Jesus reigns.

TRUSTING JESUS.

I AM trusting Thee, Lord Jesus,
 Trusting only Thee;
Trusting Thee for full salvation,
  Great and free.

I am trusting Thee for pardon;
 At Thy feet I bow,
For Thy grace and tender mercy,
  Trusting now.

I am trusting Thee for cleansing
 In the crimson flood;
Trusting Thee to make me holy
  By Thy blood.

I am trusting Thee to guide me;
 Thou alone shalt lead!
Every day and hour supplying
  All my need.

I am trusting Thee for power;
 Thine can never fail!
Words which Thou Thyself shalt give me,
  Must prevail.

I am trusting Thee, Lord Jesus:
 Never let me fall!
I am trusting Thee for ever,
  And for all.

LOOKING UNTO JESUS.

LOOKING unto Jesus!
 Battle-shout of faith,
Shield o'er all the armour,
 Free from scar or scathe.
Standard of salvation,
 In our hearts unfurled,
Let its elevation
 Overcome the world!

Look away to Jesus,
 Look away from all;
Then we need not stumble,
 Then we shall not fall.
From each snare that lureth,
 Foe or phantom grim,
Safety this ensureth:
 Look away to Him.

Looking into Jesus,
   Wonderingly we trace
Heights of power and glory,
   Depths of love and grace.
Vistas far unfolding
   Ever stretch before,
As we gaze, beholding
   Ever more and more.

Looking up to Jesus,
   On the emerald throne!
Faith shall pierce the heavens
   Where our King is gone.
Lord, on Thee depending,
   Now, continually,
Heart and mind ascending,
   Let us dwell with Thee.

RESTING.

"This is the rest wherewith ye may cause the weary to rest;
and this is the refreshing."
—ISAIAH 28:12.

RESTING on the faithfulness of Christ our Lord;
Resting on the fulness of His own sure word;
Resting on His power, on His love untold;
Resting on His covenant secured of old.

Resting 'neath His guiding hand for untracked days;
Resting 'neath His shadow from the noontide rays;
Resting at the eventide beneath His wing,
In the fair pavilion of our Saviour King.

Resting in the fortress while the foe is nigh;
Resting in the lifeboat while the waves roll high;
Resting in His chariot for the swift glad race;
Resting, always resting in His boundless grace.

Resting in the pastures, and beneath the Rock;
Resting by the waters where He leads His flock;
Resting, while we listen, at His glorious feet;
Resting in His very arms!—O rest complete!

Resting and believing, let us onward press,
Resting in Himself, the Lord our Righteousness;
Resting and rejoicing, let His saved ones sing,
Glory, glory, glory be to Christ our King!

INCREASE OUR FAITH.

"Lord, increase our faith."—LUKE 17:5.

INCREASE our faith, belovèd Lord!
   For Thou alone canst give
The faith that takes Thee at Thy word,
   The faith by which we live.

Increase our faith! So weak are we,
    That we both may and must
Commit our very faith to Thee,
    Entrust to Thee our trust.

Increase our faith! for there is yet
    Much land to be possessed;
And by no other strength we get
    Our heritage of rest.

Increase our faith! On this broad shield
    "All" fiery darts be caught;
We must be victors in the field
    Where Thou for us hast fought.

Increase our faith, that we may claim
    Each starry promise sure,
And *always* triumph in Thy name,
    And to the end endure.

Increase our faith, O Lord, we pray,
    That we may not depart
From Thy commands, but *all* obey
    With free and loyal heart.

Increase our faith—increase it still—
    From heavenward hour to hour,
And in us gloriously "fulfil
    The work of faith with power."

Increase our faith, that never dim
    Or trembling it may be,
Crowned with the "perfect peace" of him
    "Whose mind is stayed on Thee."

Increase our faith, for Thou hast prayed
    That it should never fail;
Our stedfast anchorage is made
    With Thee, within the veil.

Increase our faith, that unto Thee
    More fruit may still abound;
That it may grow "exceedingly,"
    And to Thy praise be found.

Increase our faith, O Saviour dear,
    By Thy sweet sovereign grace,
Till, changing faith for vision clear,
    We see Thee face to face!

HE IS THY LIFE.

Jesus, Thy life is mine!
Dwell evermore in me;
    And let me see
That nothing can untwine
    My life from Thine.

Thy life in me be shown!
Lord, I would henceforth seek
    To think and speak
Thy thoughts, Thy words alone,
    No more my own.

Thy love, Thy joy, Thy peace,
Continuously impart
    Unto my heart;
Fresh springs, that never cease,
    But still increase.

The blest reality
Of resurrection power,
    Thy Church's dower,
Life more abundantly,
    Lord, give to me!

Thy fullest gift, O Lord,
Now at Thy feet I claim,
    Through Thy dear name!
And touch the rapturous chord
    Of praise forth poured.

Jesus, my life is Thine,
And evermore shall be
    Hidden in Thee!
For nothing can untwine
    Thy life from mine.

ENOUGH.

I am so weak, dear Lord, I cannot stand
    One moment without Thee!
But oh! the tenderness of Thine enfolding,
And oh! the faithfulness of Thine upholding,
And oh! the strength of Thy right hand!
    That strength is enough for me!

I am so needy, Lord, and yet I know
    All fulness dwells in Thee;
And hour by hour that never-failing treasure
Supplies and fills, in overflowing measure,
My least, my greatest need; and so
    Thy grace is enough for me!

It is so sweet to trust Thy word alone:
    I do not ask to see
The unveiling of Thy purpose, or the shining
Of future light on mysteries untwining:
Thy promise-roll is all my own,—
    Thy word is enough for me!

The human heart asks love; but now I know
    That my heart hath from Thee
All real, and full, and marvellous affection,
So near, so human; yet divine perfection
Thrills gloriously the mighty glow!
    Thy love is enough for me!

There were strange soul-depths, restless, vast, and broad,
　　Unfathomed as the sea;
An infinite craving for some infinite stilling;
But now Thy perfect love is perfect filling!
Lord Jesus Christ, my Lord, my God,
　　Thou, Thou art enough for me!

"MASTER, SAY ON!"

Master, speak! Thy servant heareth,
　　Waiting for Thy gracious word,
Longing for Thy voice that cheereth;
　　Master! let it now be heard.
I am listening, Lord, for Thee;
What hast Thou to say to me?

Master, speak in love and power:
　　Crown the mercies of the day,
In this quiet evening hour
　　Of the moonrise o'er the bay,
With the music of Thy voice;
Speak! and bid Thy child rejoice.

Often through my heart is pealing
　　Many another voice than Thine,
Many an unwilled echo stealing
　　From the walls of this Thy shrine:
Let Thy longed-for accents fall;
Master, speak! and silence all.

Master, speak! I do not doubt Thee,
　　Though so tearfully I plead;
Saviour, Shepherd! oh, without Thee
　　Life would be a blank indeed!
But I long for fuller light,
Deeper love, and clearer sight.

Resting on the "faithful saying,"
　　Trusting what Thy gospel saith,
On Thy written promise staying
　　All my hope in life and death,
Yet I long for something more
From Thy love's exhaustless store.

Speak to me by name, O Master,
　　Let me *know* it is to me;
Speak, that I may follow faster,
　　With a step more firm and free,
Where the Shepherd leads the flock,
In the shadow of the Rock.

Master, speak! I kneel before Thee,
　　Listening, longing, waiting still;
Oh, how long shall I implore Thee
　　This petition to fulfil!
Hast Thou not one word for me?
Must my prayer unanswered be?

Master, speak! Though least and lowest,
　　Let me not unheard depart;
Master, speak! for oh, Thou knowest
　　All the yearning of my heart,
Knowest all its truest need;
Speak! and make me blest indeed.

Master, speak! and make me ready,
　　When Thy voice is truly heard,
With obedience glad and steady
　　Still to follow every word.
I am listening, Lord, for Thee;
Master, speak, oh, speak to me!

MY MASTER.

"I love my master; . . . I will not go out free. And he shall serve
him for ever."—EXODUS 21:5, 6.

I LOVE, I love my Master,
    I will not go out free,
For He is my Redeemer,
    He paid the price for me.

I would not leave His service,
    It is so sweet and blest;
And in the weariest moments
    He gives the truest rest.

I would not halve my service,
    His only it must be,—
His *only*, who so loved me
    And gave Himself for me.

My Master shed His life-blood
    My vassal life to win,
And save me from the bondage
    Of tyrant self and sin.

He chose me for His service,
    And gave me power to choose
That blessèd, "perfect freedom"
    Which I shall never lose:

For He hath met my longing
    With word of golden tone,
That I shall serve for ever
    Himself, Himself alone.

"Shall serve Him" hour by hour,
    For He will show me how;
My Master is fulfilling
    His promise even now!

"Shall serve Him," and "for ever";
    O hope most sure, most fair!
The perfect love outpouring
    In perfect service there!

Rejoicing and adoring,
    Henceforth my song shall be:
I love, I love my Master,
    I will not go out free!

OUR KING.

"Worship thou Him."—PSALM 45:11.

O SAVIOUR, precious Saviour,
    Whom yet unseen we love;
O Name of might and favour,
    All other names above!
      We worship Thee, we bless Thee,
        To Thee alone we sing;
      We praise Thee, and confess Thee
        Our holy Lord and King!

O Bringer of salvation,
    Who wondrously hast wrought,
Thyself the revelation
    Of love beyond our thought!
      We worship Thee, we bless Thee,
        To Thee alone we sing;
      We praise Thee, and confess Thee
        Our gracious Lord and King!

In Thee all fulness dwelleth,
   All grace and power divine;
The glory that excelleth,
   O Son of God, is Thine:
      We worship Thee, we bless Thee,
        To Thee alone we sing;
      We praise Thee, and confess Thee
        Our glorious Lord and King!

Oh, grant the consummation
   Of this our song above,
In endless adoration,
   And everlasting love:
      Then shall we praise and bless Thee,
        Where perfect praises ring,
      And evermore confess Thee
        Our Saviour and our King!

ONLY.

Only a mortal's powers,
   Weak at their fullest strength;
Only a few swift-flashing hours,
   Short at their fullest length.

Only a page for the eye,
   Only a word for the ear,
Only a smile, and by and by
   Only a quiet tear.

Only one heart to give,
   Only one voice to use;
Only one little life to live,
   And only one to lose.

Poor is my best, and small:
   How could I dare divide?
Surely my Lord shall have it all,
   He shall not be denied!

All! for far more I owe
   Than all I have to bring;
All! for my Saviour loves me so!
   All! for I love my King!

All! for it is His own,
   He gave the tiny store;
All! for it must be His alone;
   All! for I have no more.

All! for the last and least
   He stoopeth to uplift:
The altar of my great High Priest
   Shall sanctify my gift.

HOPE.

What though the blossom fall and die?
   The flower is not the root;
The sun of love may ripen yet
   The Master's pleasant fruit.

What though by many a sinful fall
    Thy garments are defiled?
A Saviour's blood can cleanse them all;
    Fear not! thou art His child.

Arise! and, leaning on His strength,
    Thy weakness shall be strong;
And He will teach Thy heart at length
    A new perpetual song.

Arise! to follow in His track
    Each holy footprint clear,
And on an upward course look back
    With every brightening year.

Arise! and on thy future way
    His blessing with thee be!
His presence be thy staff and stay,
    Till Thou His glory see.

TRUST AND DISTRUST.

DISTRUST thyself, but trust His grace;
    It is enough for thee!
In every trial thou shalt trace
    Its all-sufficiency.

Distrust thyself, but trust His strength;
    In Him thou shalt be strong:
His weakest ones may learn at length
    A daily triumph-song.

Distrust thyself, but trust His love;
    Rest in its changeless glow:
And life or death shall only prove
    Its everlasting flow.

Distrust thyself, but trust alone
    In Him, for all—for ever!
And joyously thy heart shall own
    That Jesus faileth never.

CONFIDENCE.

(IMPROMPTU ON THE ROAD TO WARWICK.)

IN Thee I trust, on Thee I rest,
O Saviour dear, Redeemer blest!
No earthly friend, no brother knows
My weariness, my wants, my woes.
      On Thee I call,
      Who knowest all.
O Saviour dear, Redeemer blest,
In Thee I trust, on Thee I rest.

Thy power, Thy love, Thy faithfulness,
With lip and life I long to bless.
Thy faithfulness shall be my tower,
My sun Thy love, my shield Thy power

In darkest night,
In fiercest fight.
With lip and life I long to bless
Thy power, Thy love, Thy faithfulness.

REST.

"Thou hast made us for Thyself, and the heart never resteth till it findeth
rest in Thee."—St. Augustine.

MADE for Thyself, O God!
Made for Thy love, Thy service, Thy delight;
Made to show forth Thy wisdom, grace, and might;
Made for Thy praise, whom veiled archangels laud;
Oh strange and glorious thought, that we may be
A joy to Thee!

Yet the heart turns away
From this grand destiny of bliss, and deems
'Twas made for its poor self, for passing dreams,
Chasing illusions melting day by day;
Till *for ourselves* we read on this world's best,
"This is not rest!"

Nor can the vain toil cease,
Till in the shadowy maze of life we meet
One who can guide our aching, wayward feet
To find Himself, our Way, our Life, our Peace.
In Him the long unrest is soothed and stilled;
Our hearts are filled.

O rest, so true, so sweet!
(Would it were shared by all the weary world!)
'Neath shadowing banner of His love unfurled,
We bend to kiss the Master's piercèd feet;
Then lean our love upon His loving breast,
And know God's rest.

CHRISTMAS VERSES.

These are three single verses on Christmas by F.R.H.:

OH, Christmas blessings cannot cease,
Christmas joy is deep and strong!
For Christ is come to be our Peace,
Our Salvation and our Song.

"Behold, thy King cometh unto thee."—ZECHARIAH 9:9.

COMETH in lowliness,
Cometh in righteousness,
Cometh in mercy all royal and free!
Cometh with grace and might,
Cometh with love and light;
Cometh, belovèd! He cometh to thee!

WHAT was the first angelic word
That the startled shepherds heard?—
"Fear not!" Beloved, it comes to you
As a Christmas message most sweet and true,
As true for you as it was for them
In the lonely fields of Bethlehem;
And as sweet to-day as it was that night,
When the glory dazzled their mortal sight.

MATTHEW 14:23.

"And when he had sent the multitudes away, he went up into a mountain
apart to pray: and when the evening was come, he was there alone."

IT is the quiet evening time, the sun is in the west,
And earth enrobed in purple glow awaits her nightly rest;
The shadows of the mountain peaks are lengthening o'er the sea,
And the flowerets close their eyelids on the shore of Galilee.
The multitude are gone away, their restless hum doth cease,
The birds have hushed their music, and all is calm and peace;
But on the lowly mountain side is One, whose beauteous brow
The impress bears of sorrow and of weariness e'en now.
The livelong day in deeds of love and power He hath spent,
And with them words of grace and life hath ever sweetly blent.
Now He hath gained the mountain top, He standeth all alone,
No mortal may be near Him in that hour of prayer unknown.
He prayeth.—But for whom? For Himself He needeth nought;
Nor strength, nor peace, nor pardon, where of sin there is no spot;
But 'tis for us in powerful prayer He spendeth all the night,
That His own loved ones may be kept and strengthened in the fight;
That they may all be sanctified, and perfect made in one;
That they His glory may behold where they shall need no sun;
That in eternal gladness they may be His glorious bride:
It is for this that He hath climbed the lonely mountain side.
It is for this that He denies His weary head the rest
Which e'en the foxes in their holes, and birds have in their nest.
The echo of that prayer hath died upon the rocky hill,
But on a higher, holier mount that Voice is pleading still;

For while one weary child of His yet wanders here below,
While yet one thirsting soul desires His peace and love to know,
And while one fainting spirit seeks His holiness to share,
The Saviour's loving heart shall pour a tide of mighty prayer;
Yes! till each ransomed one hath gained His home of joy and peace,
That Fount of Blessings all untold shall never, never cease.

ACCEPTED.

"Accepted in the Beloved."—EPHESIANS 1:6. "Perfect in Christ Jesus."
—COLOSSIANS 1:28. "Complete in Him."—COLOSSIANS 2:10.

ACCEPTED, Perfect, and Complete,
For God's inheritance made meet!
How true, how glorious, and how sweet!

In the Belovèd—by the King
Accepted, though not anything
But forfeit lives had we to bring.

And Perfect in Christ Jesus made,
On Him our great transgressions laid,
We in His righteousness arrayed.

Complete in Him, our glorious Head,
With Jesus raisèd from the dead,
And by His mighty Spirit led!

O blessèd Lord, is this for me?
Then let my whole life henceforth be
One Alleluia-song to Thee!

COVENANT BLESSINGS.

"He hath made with me an everlasting covenant, ordered in all things,
and sure."—2 SAMUEL 23:5.

JEHOVAH'S Covenant shall endure,
All ordered, everlasting, sure!
O child of God, rejoice to trace
Thy portion in its glorious grace.

'Tis thine, for Christ is given to be
The Covenant of God to thee:
In Him, God's golden scroll of light,
The darkest truths are clear and bright.

O sorrowing sinner, well He knew,
Ere time began, what He would do!
Then rest thy hope within the veil;
His covenant mercies shall not fail.

O doubting one, the Eternal Three
Are pledged in faithfulness for thee;
Claim every promise, sweet and sure,
By covenant oath of God secure.

O waiting one, each moment's fall
Is marked by love that planned them all;
Thy times, all ordered by His hand,
In God's eternal covenant stand.

O feeble one, look up and see
Strong consolation sworn for thee;
Jehovah's glorious arm is shown,
His covenant strength is all thine own.

O mourning one, each stroke of love
A covenant blessing yet shall prove;
His covenant love shall be thy stay;
His covenant grace be as thy day.

O Love that chose, O Love that died,
O Love that sealed and sanctified!
All glory, glory, glory be,
O covenant Triune God, to Thee!

IS IT FOR ME?

"O Thou whom my soul loveth."—SONG OF SOLOMON 1:7.

Is it for me, dear Saviour,
　　Thy glory and Thy rest?
For me, so weak and sinful,
　　Oh, shall *I* thus be blessed?
Is it for me to see Thee
　　In all Thy glorious grace,
And gaze in endless rapture
　　On Thy belovèd Face?

Is it for me to listen
　　To Thy belovèd Voice,
And hear its sweetest music
　　Bid even me rejoice?
Is it for me, Thy welcome,
　　Thy gracious "Enter in"?
For me, Thy "Come, ye blessed!"
　　For me, so full of sin?

O Saviour, precious Saviour,
　　My heart is at Thy feet;
I bless Thee and I love Thee,
　　And Thee I long to meet.
A thrill of solemn gladness
　　Has hushed my very heart,
To think that I shall really
　　Behold Thee as Thou art;

Behold Thee in Thy beauty,
　　Behold Thee face to face;
Behold Thee in Thy glory,
　　And reap Thy smile of grace;
And be with Thee for ever,
　　And never grieve Thee more!
Dear Saviour, I *must* praise Thee,
　　And lovingly adore.

ISAIAH 33:17.

THINE eyes shall see! Yes, thine, who, blind erewhile,
 Now trembling towards the new-found light dost flee,
Leave doubting, and look up with trustful smile—
   Thine eyes shall see!

Thine *eyes* shall see! Not in some dream Elysian,
 Not in thy fancy, glowing though it be,
Not e"en in faith, but in unveilèd vision,
   Thine *eyes* shall see!

Thine eyes *shall* see! Not on thyself depend
 God's promises, the faithful, firm, and free;
Ere they shall fail, earth, heaven itself, must end:
   Thine eyes *shall* see!

Thine eyes shall *see!* Not in a swift glance cast,
 Gleaning one ray to brighten memory,
But while a glad eternity shall last,
   Thine eyes shall *see!*

Thine eyes shall see *the* King! The very same
 Whose love shone forth upon the curseful tree,
Who bore thy guilt, who calleth thee by name;
   Thine eyes shall see!

Thine eyes shall see the *King!* the mighty One,
 The many-crowned, the Light-enrobed; and He
Shall bid thee share the kingdom He hath won,
   Thine eyes shall see!

 And *in His beauty!* Stay thee, mortal song,
  The "altogether lovely" One must be
 Unspeakable in glory,—yet ere long
   Thine eyes shall see!

 Yes! though the land be "very far" away,
  A step, a moment, ends the toil for thee;
 Then, changing grief for gladness, night for day,
   Thine eyes shall see!

THE SOVEREIGNTY OF GOD.

"Be still, and know that I am God."—PSALM 46:10.

GOD Almighty! King of nations! earth Thy footstool, heaven Thy throne!
Thine the greatness, power, and glory, Thine the kingdom, Lord, alone!
Life and death are in Thy keeping, and Thy will ordaineth all,
From the armies of Thy heavens to an unseen insect's fall.

Reigning, guiding, all-commanding, ruling myriad worlds of light;
Now exalting, now abasing, none can stay Thy hand of might!
Working all things by Thy power, by the counsel of Thy will,
Thou art God! enough to know it, and to hear Thy word: "Be still!"

In Thy sovereignty rejoicing, we Thy children bow and praise,
For we know that kind and loving, just and true, are all Thy ways.
While Thy heart of sovereign mercy and Thine arm of sovereign might,
For our great and strong salvation, in Thy sovereign grace unite.

GOD THE PROVIDER.

"My God shall supply all your need, according to His riches in glory by
Christ Jesus."—PHILIPPIANS 4:19.

WHO shall tell our untold need,
    Deeply felt, though scarcely known!
Who the hungering soul can feed,
    Guard, and guide, but God alone?
Blessèd promise! while we see
Earthly friends must powerless be,
Earthly fountains quickly dry:
"*God*" shall all your need supply.

He hath said it! so we know
    Nothing less can we receive.
Oh that thankful love may glow
    While we restfully believe,—
Ask not *how,* but trust Him still;
Ask not *when,* but wait His will:
Simply on His word rely,
God "*shall*" all your need supply.

Through the whole of life's long way,
    Outward, inward need we trace;
Need arising day by day,
    Patience, wisdom, strength, and grace.
Needing Jesus most of all,
Full of need, on Him we call;
Then how gracious His reply,
God shall "*all*" your need supply!

Great our need, but greater far
    Is our Father's loving power;
He upholds each mighty star,
    He unfolds each tiny flower.
He who numbers every hair,
Earnest of His faithful care,
Gave His Son for us to die;
God shall all "*your*" need supply.

Yet we often vainly plead
    For a fancied good denied,
What we deemed a pressing need
    Still remaining unsupplied.
Yet from dangers all concealed,
Thus our wisest Friend doth shield;
No *good* thing will He deny,
God shall all your *"need"* supply.

Can we count redemption's treasure,
    Scan the glory of God's love?
Such shall be the boundless measure
    Of His blessings from above.
All we ask or think, and more,
He will give in bounteous store,—
He can fill and satisfy!
God shall all your need *"supply."*[1]

One the channel, deep and broad,
    From the Fountain of the Throne,
Christ the Saviour, Son of God,
    Blessings flow through Him alone.
He, the Faithful and the True,
Brings us mercies ever new:
Till we reach His home on high,
"God shall all your need supply."

THE UNFAILING ONE.

"He faileth not."—ZEPHANIAH 3:5.

HE who hath led will lead
    All through the wilderness;
He who hath fed will feed;
    He who hath blessed will bless;
He who hath heard thy cry,
    Will never close His ear;
He who hath marked thy faintest sigh,
    Will not forget thy tear.
He loveth always, faileth never;
So rest on Him, to-day, for ever!

He who hath made thee whole
    Will heal thee day by day;
He who hath spoken to thy soul
    Hath many things to say.

---

[1] The Greek word is much stronger than the English,—πληρώσει—"will supply to the full," "fill up," "satisfy."

He who hath gently taught
　　Yet more will make thee know;
He who so wondrously hath wrought
　　Yet greater things will show.
He loveth always, faileth never;
So rest on Him, to-day, for ever!

He who hath made thee nigh
　　Will draw thee nearer still;
He who hath given the first supply
　　Will satisfy and fill.
He who hath given thee grace
　　Yet more and more will send;
He who hath set thee in the race
　　Will speed thee to the end.
He loveth always, faileth never;
So rest on Him, to-day, for ever!

He who hath won thy heart
　　Will keep it true and free;
He who hath shown thee what thou art
　　Will show Himself to thee.
He who hath bid thee live,
　　And made thy life His own,
Life more abundantly will give,
　　And keep it His alone.
He loveth always, faileth never;
So rest on Him, to-day, for ever!

Then trust Him for to-day
　　As thine unfailing Friend,
And let Him lead thee all the way,
　　Who loveth to the end.
And let the morrow rest
　　In His belovèd hand;
His good is better than our best,
　　As we shall understand,—
If, trusting Him who faileth never,
We rest on Him, to-day, for ever!

THIS SAME JESUS.

Acts i:11.

"This same Jesus!" Oh! how sweetly
　　Fall those words upon the ear,
Like a swell of far off music,
　　In a nightwatch still and drear!

He who healed the hopeless leper,
　　He who dried the widow's tear;
He who changed to health and gladness
　　Helpless suffering, trembling fear;

He who wandered, poor and homeless,
　　By the stormy Galilee;
He who on the night-robed mountain
　　Bent in prayer the wearied knee;

He who spake as none had spoken,
　　Angel-wisdom far above,
All-forgiving, ne'er upbraiding,
　　Full of tenderness and love;

He who gently called the weary,
　　"Come and I will give you rest!"
He who loved the little children,
　　Took them in His arms and blest;

He, the lonely Man of sorrows,
　　'Neath our sin-curse bending low;
By His faithless friends forsaken
　　In the darkest hours of woe;—

"This *same* Jesus!" When the vision
　　Of that last and awful day
Bursts upon the prostrate spirit,
　　Like a midnight lightning ray;

When, else dimly apprehended,
　　All its terrors seem revealed,
Trumpet knell and fiery heavens,
　　And the books of doom unsealed;

Then, we lift our hearts adoring
　　"This same Jesus," loved and known,
Him, our own most gracious Saviour,
　　Seated on the great white Throne;

He Himself, and "not another,"
　　He for whom our heart-love yearned
Through long years of twilight waiting,
　　To His ransomed ones returned!

For this word, O Lord, we bless Thee,
　　Bless our Master's changeless name;
Yesterday, to-day, for ever,
　　Jesus Christ is still the Same.

THE TRIUNE PRESENCE.

(Birthday or New Year's hymn.)

"Certainly I will be with thee."—Exodus 3:12.

"Certainly I will be with thee!" Father, I have found it true:
To Thy faithfulness and mercy I would set my seal anew.
All the year Thy grace hath kept me, Thou my help indeed hast been,
Marvellous the loving-kindness every day and hour hath seen.

"Certainly I will be with thee!" Let me feel it, Saviour dear,
Let me know that Thou art with me, very precious, very near.
On this day of solemn pausing, with Thyself all longing still,
Let Thy pardon, let Thy presence, let Thy peace my spirit fill.

"Certainly I will be with thee!" Blessèd Spirit, come to me,
Rest upon me, dwell within me, let my heart Thy temple be;
Through the trackless year before me, Holy One, with me Abide!
Teach me, comfort me, and calm me, be my ever-present Guide.

"Certainly I will be with thee!" Starry promise in the night!
All uncertainties, like shadows, flee away before its light.
"Certainly I will be with thee!" He hath spoken: I have heard!
True of old, and true this moment, I will trust Jehovah's word.

FEAR NOT.

Isaiah 43:1–7.

Listen! for the Lord hath spoken!
  "Fear thou not," saith He;
"When thou passest through the waters,
  I will be with thee.

"Fear not! for I have redeemed thee;
  All My sheep I know!
When thou passest through the rivers,
  They shall not o"erflow.

"Fear not! by thy name I called thee,—
  Mine thy heart hath learned;
When thou walkest through the fire,
  Thou shalt not be burned.

"Thou art Mine! oh, therefore fear not!
  Mine for ever now!
And the flame shall never kindle
  On thy sealèd brow.

"Thou art precious, therefore fear not,
  Precious unto Me!
I have made thee for My glory,
  I have lovèd thee."

TINY TOKENS.

THE murmur of a waterfall
    A mile away,
The rustle when a robin lights
    Upon a spray,
The lapping of a lowland stream
    On dipping boughs,
The sound of grazing from a herd
    Of gentle cows,
The echo from a wooded hill
    Of cuckoo's call,
The quiver through the meadow grass
    At evening fall:—
Too subtle are these harmonies
    For pen and rule,
Such music is not understood
    By any school:
But when the brain is overwrought,
    It hath a spell,
Beyond all human skill and power,
    To make it well.

The memory of a kindly word
    For long gone by,
The fragrance of a fading flower
    Sent lovingly,
The gleaming of a sudden smile
    Or sudden tear,
The warmer pressure of the hand,
    The tone of cheer,
The hush that means "I cannot speak,
    But I have heard!"
The note that only bears a verse
    From God's own Word:—
Such tiny things we hardly count
    As ministry;
The givers deeming they have shown
    Scant sympathy:
But when the heart is overwrought,
    Oh, who can tell
The power of such tiny things
    To make it well!

ASKING: (FOR WHIT-SUNDAY).

"If ye then, being evil, know how to give good gifts unto your children:
how much more shall your Heavenly Father give the Holy Spirit
to them that ask Him?"—St. LUKE 11:13.

O HEAVENLY Father, Thou hast told
Of a Gift more precious than pearls and gold;
A Gift that is free to every one,
Through Jesus Christ, Thy only Son:
    For His sake, give it to me!

Oh, give it to me, for Jesus said
That a father giveth his children bread:
And how much more Thou wilt surely give
The Gift by which the dead shall live!
    For Christ's sake, give it to me!

I cannot see, and I want the sight:
I am in the dark, and I want the light;
I want to pray, and I don't know how;
Oh, give me Thy Holy Spirit now!
    For Christ's sake, give it to me!

If Thou hast said it, I must believe,
It is only "ask" and I shall receive;
If Thou hast said it, it must be true,
And there's nothing else for me to do!
    For Christ's sake, give it to me!

So I come and ask, because my need
Is very great and real indeed.
On the strength of Thy Word I come and say,
Oh, let Thy Word come true to-day!
    For Christ's sake, give it to me!

NEW YEAR'S WISHES.

WHAT shall I wish thee?
    Treasures of earth?
Songs in the spring-time,
    Pleasure and mirth?
Flowers on thy pathway,
    Skies ever clear?
Would this ensure thee
    A Happy New Year?

What shall I wish thee?
    What can be found
Bringing thee sunshine
    All the year round?
Where is the treasure,
    Lasting and dear,
That shall ensure thee
    A Happy New Year?

Faith that increaseth,
    Walking in light;
Hope that aboundeth,
    Happy and bright;
Love that is perfect,
    Casting out fear;—
These shall ensure thee
    A Happy New Year.

Peace in the Saviour,
    Rest at His feet,
Smile of His countenance
    Radiant and sweet,
Joy in His presence,
    Christ ever near!—
This will ensure thee
    A Happy New Year!

FAITHFUL PROMISES.

NEW YEAR'S HYMN. ISAIAH 41:10.

STANDING at the portal
    Of the opening year,
Words of comfort meet us,
    Hushing every fear.
Spoken through the silence
    By our Father's voice,
Tender, strong, and faithful,
    Making us rejoice.
      Onward, then, and fear not,
        Children of the Day!
    For His word shall never,
      Never pass away!

I, the Lord, am with thee,
    Be thou not afraid!
I will help and strengthen,
    Be thou not dismayed!
Yea, I will uphold thee
    With My own Right Hand;
Thou art called and chosen
    In my sight to stand.
      Onward, then, and fear not,
        Children of the Day!
    For His word shall never,
      Never pass away!

For the year before us,
   Oh, what rich supplies!
For the poor and needy
   Living streams shall rise;
For the sad and sinful
   Shall His grace abound;
For the faint and feeble
   Perfect strength be found.
     Onward, then, and fear not,
      Children of the Day!
     For His word shall never,
      Never pass away!

He will never fail us,
   He will not forsake;
His eternal covenant
   He will never break!
Resting on His promise,
   What have we to fear?
God is all-sufficient
   For the coming year.
     Onward, then, and fear not.
      Children of the Day!
     For His word shall never,
      Never pass away!

I COULD NOT DO WITHOUT THEE.

I COULD not do without Thee,
   O Saviour of the lost!
Whose precious blood redeemed me,
   At such tremendous cost.
Thy righteousness, Thy pardon,
   Thy precious blood must be
My only hope and comfort,
   My glory and my plea!

I could not do without Thee!
   I cannot stand alone,
I have no strength or goodness,
   No wisdom of my own.
But Thou, belovèd Saviour,
   Art all in all to me;
And weakness will be power,
   If leaning hard on Thee.

I could not do without Thee!
   For oh! the way is long,
And I am often weary,
   And sigh replaces song.
How *could* I do without Thee?
   I do not know the way;
Thou knowest and Thou leadest,
   And wilt not let me stray.

I could not do without Thee,
   O Jesus, Saviour dear!
E'en when my eyes are holden,
   I know that Thou art near.
How dreary and how lonely
   This changeful life would be,
Without the sweet communion,
   The secret rest with Thee!

I could not do without Thee!
   No other friend can read
The spirit's strange deep longings,
   Interpreting its need.
No human heart could enter
   Each dim recess of mine,
And soothe and hush and calm it,
   O blessèd Lord, but Thine!

I could not do without Thee!
   For years are fleeting fast,
And soon, in solemn loneliness,
   The river must be passed.
But Thou wilt never leave me,
   And, though the waves roll high,
I know Thou wilt be near me,
   And whisper, " It is I."

THE SONG OF A SUMMER STREAM.

A FEW months ago
I was singing through the snow,
Though the dead brown boughs gave no hope of summer shoots,
And my persevering fall
Seemed to be no use at all,
For the hard, hard frost would not let me reach the roots.

Then the mists hung chill
All along the wooded hill,
And the cold, sad fog through my lonely dingles crept;
I was glad I had no power
To awake one tender flower
To a sure, swift doom! I would rather that it slept.

Still I sang all alone
In the sweet old summer tone,
For the strong white ice could not hush me for a day;
Though no other voice was heard
But the bitter breeze that whirred
Past the gaunt, grey trunks on its wild and angry way.

So the dim days sped,
While everything seemed dead,
And my own poor flow seemed the only living sign;
And the keen stars shone
When the freezing night came on,
From the far, far heights, all so cold and crystalline.

A few months ago
I was singing through the snow!
But now the blessed sunshine is filling all the land,
And the memories are lost
Of the winter fog and frost,
In the presence of the Summer with her full and glowing hand.

Now the woodlark comes to drink
At my cool and pearly brink,
And the ladyfern is bending to kiss my rainbow foam;
And the wild-rose buds entwine
With the dark-leaved bramble-vine,
And the centuried oak is green around the bright-eyed squirrel's home.

O the full and glad content,
That my little song is blent
With the all-melodious mingling of the choristers around!
I no longer sing alone
Through a chill surrounding moan,
For the very air is trembling with its wealth of summer sound.

Though the hope seemed long deferred,
Ere the south wind's whisper heard
Gave a promise of the passing of the weary winter days,
Yet the blessing was secure,
For the summer time was sure
When the lonely songs are gathered in the mighty choir of praise.

A PRAYER.

This poem was written by F.R.H. in 1849, when she was twelve.

LORD, in mercy pardon me
All that I this day have done:
Sins of every kind 'gainst Thee,
O forgive them through Thy Son.

Make me, Jesus, like to Thee,
Gentle, holy, meek, and mild,
My transgressions pardon me,
O forgive a sinful child.

Gracious Spirit, listen Thou,
Enter in my willing heart,
Enter and possess it now,
Never, Lord, from me depart.

O eternal Three in One,
Condescend to bend Thine ear;
Help me still towards heaven to run,
Answer now my humble prayer.

JESSIE'S FRIEND.

This poem was written for children.

LITTLE Jessie, darling pet,
Do you want a Friend?
One who never will forget,
Loving to the end;
One whom you can tell when sad
Everything that grieves;
One who loves to make you glad,
One who never leaves.

Such a loving Friend is ours,
Near us all the day,
Helping us in lesson hours,
Smiling on our play;
Keeping us from doing wrong,
Guarding everywhere,
Listening to each happy song
And each little prayer.

Jessie, if you only knew
What He is to me,
Surely you would seek Him too,
You would "come and see."
Come, and you will find it true,
Happy you will be;
Jesus says, and says to you,
"Come, oh come to Me."

EVENING PRAYER.

This is another poem written for children.

Now the light has gone away,
    Saviour, listen while I pray,
Asking Thee to watch and keep,
    And to send me quiet sleep.

Jesus, Saviour, wash away
    All that has been wrong to-day,
Help me every day to be
    Good and gentle, more like Thee.

Let my near and dear ones be
    Always near and dear to Thee;
Oh, bring me and all I love
    To Thy happy home above!

Now my evening praise I give:
    Thou didst die that I might live,
All my blessings come from Thee;
    Oh, how good Thou art to me!

Thou, my best and kindest Friend,
    Thou wilt love me to the end!
Let me love Thee more and more,
    Always better than before!

MY LITTLE TREE.

This is another poem written for children.

THEY tell me that my little tree
Is only just my age, but see,—
Already ripe and rosy fruit
Is peeping under every shoot!
How little have I brought,
But withered leaves of foolish thought;
And angry words, like thorn,
How many have I borne!

No fruit my little tree can bring
Without the gentle rain of spring;
Nor could it ever ripen one,
Without the glowing summer sun:
O Father! shed on me
Thy Holy Spirit from above,
That I may bring to Thee
The golden fruit of love.

Let sunshine of Thy grace increase
The pleasant fruit of joy and peace,
With purple gleam of gentleness,
That most of all my home may bless;
While faith and goodness meet
In ruby ripeness rich and sweet,
Let these in me be found,
And evermore abound.

WHO WILL TAKE CARE OF ME?

This poem was written for a friend's daughter.

WRITTEN FOR EMILY F. W. W. SNEPP.

WHO will take care of me? darling, you say!
    Lovingly, tenderly watched as you are!
Listen! I give you the answer to-day,
    ONE who is never forgetful or far!

He will take care of you! all through the day,
    Jesus is near you to keep you from ill;
Walking or resting, at lessons or play,
    Jesus is with you and watching you still.

He will take care of you! all through the night,
    Jesus, the Shepherd, His little one keeps;
Darkness to Him is the same as the light;
    He never slumbers and He never sleeps.

He will take care of you! all through the year,
    Crowning each day with His kindness and love,
Sending you blessing and shielding from fear,
    Leading you on to the bright home above.

He will take care of you! yes, to the end!
    Nothing can alter His love to His own.
Darling, be glad that you have such a Friend,
    He will not leave you one moment alone!

JUST WHEN THOU WILT.

JUST when Thou wilt, O Master, call!
Or at the noon, or evening fall,
Or in the dark, or in the light,—
Just when Thou wilt, it must be right.

Just when Thou wilt, O Saviour, come,
Take me to dwell in Thy bright home!
Or when the snows have crowned my head,
Or ere it hath one silver thread.

Just when Thou wilt, O Bridegroom, say,
"Rise up, my love, and come away!"
Open to me Thy golden gate
Just when Thou wilt, or soon, or late.

Just when Thou wilt—Thy time is best—
Thou shalt appoint my hour of rest,

Marked by the Sun of perfect love,
Shining unchangeably above.

Just when Thou wilt!—no choice for me!
Life is a gift to use for Thee;
Death is a hushed and glorious tryst,
With Thee, my King, my Saviour, Christ!

HAVE YOU NOT A WORD FOR JESUS?

"O Lord, open Thou my lips; and my mouth shall show forth
Thy praise."—PSALM 51:15.

HAVE you not a word for Jesus? not a word to say for Him?
He is listening through the chorus of the burning seraphim!
HE IS LISTENING; does He hear you speaking of the things of earth,
Only of its passing pleasure, selfish sorrow, empty mirth?
He has spoken words of blessing, pardon, peace, and love to you,
Glorious hopes and gracious comfort, strong and tender, sweet and true;
Does He hear you telling others something of His love untold,
Overflowing of thanksgiving for His mercies manifold?

Have you not a word for Jesus? Will the world His praise proclaim?
Who shall speak if ye are silent? ye who know and love His name.
You, whom He hath called and chosen His own witnesses to be,
Will you tell your gracious Master, "Lord, we cannot speak for Thee"?
"Cannot!" though He suffered for you, died because He loved you so!
"Cannot!" though He has forgiven, making scarlet white as snow!
"Cannot!" though His grace abounding is your freely promised aid!
"Cannot!" though HE stands beside you, though HE says, "Be not afraid!"

Have you not a word for Jesus? Some, perchance, while ye are dumb,
Wait and weary for your message, hoping *you* will bid them "come";
Never telling hidden sorrows, lingering just outside the door,
Longing for *your* hand to lead them into rest for evermore.
Yours may be the joy and honour His redeemèd ones to bring,
Jewels for the coronation of your coming Lord and King.
Will you cast away the gladness thus your Master's joy to share,
All because a word for Jesus seems too much for you to dare?

What shall be our word for Jesus? Master, give it day by day;
Ever as the need arises, teach Thy children what to say.
Give us holy love and patience; grant us deep humility,
That of self we may be emptied, and our hearts be full of Thee;
Give us zeal and faith and fervour, make us winning, make us wise,
Single-hearted, strong and fearless,—Thou hast called us, we will rise!
Let the might of Thy good Spirit go with every loving word;
And by hearts prepared and opened be our message always heard!

Yes, we have a word for Jesus! Living echoes we will be
Of Thine own sweet words of blessing, of Thy gracious " Come to Me."
Jesus, Master! yes, we love Thee, and to prove our love, would lay
Fruit of lips which Thou wilt open, at Thy blessèd feet to-day.
Many an effort it may cost us, many a heart-beat, many a fear,
But Thou knowest, and wilt strengthen, and Thy help is always near.
Give us grace to follow fully, vanquishing our faithless shame,
Feebly it may be, but truly, witnessing for Thy dear Name.

Yes, we have a word for Jesus! we will bravely speak for Thee,
And Thy bold and faithful soldiers, Saviour, we would henceforth be:
In Thy name set up our banners, while Thine own shall wave above,
With Thy crimson Name of Mercy, and Thy golden Name of Love.
Help us lovingly to labour, looking for Thy present smile,
Looking for Thy promised blessing, through the brightening " little while."
Words for Thee in weakness spoken, Thou wilt here accept and own,
And confess them in Thy glory, when we see Thee on Thy throne.

OUR COMMISSION.

"And the Spirit and the Bride say, Come. And let him that heareth say, Come."
—REVELATION 22:17.

YE who hear the blessèd call
    Of the Spirit and the Bride,
Hear the Master's word to all,
    Your commission and your guide—
"And let him that heareth say,
Come," to all yet far away.

"Come!" alike to age and youth;
    Tell them of our Friend above,
Of His beauty and His truth,
    Preciousness and grace and love;
Tell them what you know is true,
Tell them what He is to you.

"Come!" to those who never heard
    Why the Saviour's blood was shed;
Bear to them the message-word
    That can quicken from the dead;
Tell them Jesus "died for all,"
Tell them of His loving call.

"Come!" to those who do not care
    For the Saviour's precious death,
Having not a thought to spare
    For the gracious words He saith:
Ere the shadows gather deep,
Rouse them from their fatal sleep.

"Come!" to those who, while they hear,
    Linger, hardly knowing why;
Tell them that the Lord is near,
    Tell them Jesus passes by.
Call them now; oh, do not wait,
Lest to-morrow be too late!

"Come!" to those who wander far,
    Seeking, never finding, rest;
Point them to the Morning Star;
    Show them how they may be blest
With the love that cannot cease,
Joyful hope and perfect peace.

"Come!" to those who draw in vain
    From the broken cisterns here,
Drinking but to thirst again;
    Tell them of the fountain near.
Living water, flowing still,
Free for "whosoever will."

"Come!" to those who faint and groan
    Under some unuttered grief,
Hearts that suffer all alone;
    Try to bring them true relief.
Tell them "Jesus wept," and He
Still is full of sympathy.

"Come!" to those who feel their sin,
    Fearing to be lost at last,
Mourning for the plague within,
    Mourning for transgressions past;
Tell them Jesus calls them in,
Heavy laden with their sin.

Such as these are all around,
    Meeting, passing, every day;
Ye who know the joyful sound,
    Have ye not a word to say?
Ye who hear that blessed "Come,"
Sweet and clear, can ye be dumb?

Brothers, sisters, do not wait,
    Speak for Him who speaks to you!
Wherefore should you hesitate?
    This is no great thing to do.
Jesus only bids you say,
"Come!" and will you not obey?

Lord! to Thy command we bow,
    Touch our lips with altar fire;
Let Thy Spirit kindle now
    Faith and zeal, and strong desire;
So that henceforth we may be
Fellow-workers, Lord, with Thee.

"JESUS ONLY."

MATTHEW 17:8.

"Jesus only!" In the shadow
    Of the cloud so chill and dim,
We are clinging, loving, trusting,
    He with us, and we with Him;
All unseen, though ever nigh,
"Jesus only"—all our cry.

"Jesus only!" In the glory,
    When the shadows all are flown,
Seeing Him in all His beauty,
    Satisfied with Him alone;
May we join His ransomed throng,
"Jesus only"—all our song!

THE ONE REALITY.

FOG-WREATHS of doubt in blinding eddies drifted,
    Whirlwinds of fancy, countergusts of thought,
    Shadowless shadows where warm lives were sought,
Numb feet, that feel not their own tread, uplifted
On clouds of formless wonder, lightning-drifted!
    What marvel that the whole world's life should seem,
    To helpless intellect, a Brahma-dream,
From which the real and restful is out-sifted!
    Through the dim storm a white peace-bearing Dove
Gleams, and the mist rolls back, the shadows flee,
    The dream is past. A clear calm sky above,
Firm rock beneath; a royal-scrollèd tree,
    And One, thorn-diademed, the King of Love,
The Son of God, who gave Himself for me.

REALITY.

"Father, we know the REALITY of Jesus Christ."
—*Words used by a workman in prayer.*

Reality, reality,
　Lord Jesus Christ, Thou art to me!
From the spectral mists and driving clouds,
From the shifting shadows and phantom crowds;
From unreal words and unreal lives,
Where truth with falsehood feebly strives;
From the passings away, the chance and change,
Flickerings, vanishings, swift and strange,
　　I turn to my glorious rest on Thee,
　　Who art the grand Reality.

Reality in greatest need,
　Lord Jesus Christ, Thou art indeed!
Is the pilot real, who alone can guide
The drifting ship through the midnight tide?
Is the lifeboat real, as it nears the wreck,
And the saved ones leap from the parting deck?
Is the haven real, where the barque may flee
From the autumn gales of the wild North Sea?
　　Reality indeed art Thou,
　　My Pilot, Lifeboat, Haven now!

Reality, reality,
　In brightest days art Thou to me!
Thou art the sunshine of my mirth,
Thou art the heaven above my earth,
The spring of the love of all my heart,
And the Fountain of my song Thou art;
For dearer than the dearest now,
And better than the best, art Thou,
　　Belovèd Lord, in whom I see
　　Joy-giving, glad Reality.

Reality, reality,
　Lord Jesus, Thou hast been to me.
When I thought the dream of life was past,
And "the Master's home-call" come at last;
When I thought I only had to wait
A little while at the Golden Gate,—
Only another day or two,
Till Thou Thyself shouldst bear me through,
　　How real Thy presence was to me
　　How precious Thy Reality!

Reality, reality,
　Lord Jesus Christ, Thou art to me!
Thy name is sweeter than songs of old,
Thy words are better than "most fine gold,"

Thy deeds are greater than hero-glory,
Thy life is grander than poet-story;
But Thou, Thyself, for aye the same,
Art more than words and life and name!
 Thyself Thou hast revealed to me,
  In glorious Reality.

  Reality, reality,
 Lord Jesus Christ, is crowned in Thee.
In Thee is every type fulfilled,
In Thee is every yearning stilled
For perfect beauty, truth, and love;
For Thou art always far above
The grandest glimpse of our Ideal,
Yet more and more we know Thee real,
  And marvel more and more to see
  Thine infinite Reality.

  Reality, reality
 Of grace and glory dwells in Thee.
How real Thy mercy and Thy might!
How real Thy love, how real Thy light!
How real Thy truth and faithfulness!
How real Thy blessing when Thou dost bless!
How real Thy coming to dwell within!
How real the triumphs Thou dost win!
  Does not the loving and glowing heart
  Leap up to own how real Thou art?

  Reality, reality!
 Such let our adoration be!
Father, we bless Thee with heart and voice,
For the wondrous grace of Thy sovereign choice.
That patiently, gently, sought us out
In the far-off land of death and doubt,
That drew us to Christ by the Spirit's might,
That opened our eyes to see the light
  That arose in strange reality,
  From the darkness falling on Calvary.

  Reality, reality,
 Lord Jesus Christ, Thou art to me!
My glorious King, my Lord, my God,
Life is too short for half the laud,
For half the debt of praise I owe
For this blest knowledge, that "I know
The reality of Jesus Christ,"—
Unmeasured blessing, gift unpriced!
  Will I not praise Thee when I see
  In the long noon of Eternity,
  Unveiled, Thy "bright Reality!"

II. EXCERPTS FROM LETTERS
AND OTHER ITEMS

[1]I had hoped that a kind of table-land had been reached in my journey, where I might walk awhile in the light, without the weary succession of rock and hollow, crag and morass, stumbling and striving; but I seem borne back into all the old difficulties of the way, with many sin-made aggravations. I think the great root of all my trouble and alienation, is that I do not now make an unreserved surrender of myself to God; and until this is done I shall know no peace. I am sure of it. I have so much to regret: a greater dread of the opinion of worldly friends, a loving of the world, and proportionate cooling in heavenly desire and love. A power utterly new and unexpected was given me (singing and composition of music), and rejoicing in this I forgot the Giver, and found such delight in this that other things paled before it. It need not have been so; and, in better moments, I prayed that if it were indeed hindering me the gift of song might be withdrawn. And now that through my ill health it is so, and that the pleasure of public applause when singing in the Philharmonic concerts is not again to exercise its delicious delusion, I do thank Him who heard my prayer. But I often pray in the dark, as it were, and feel no response from above. Is this to test me? Oh that I may be preserved from giving up in despair, and yielding, as I so often do, to the floodtide enemy.

I want to make the most of my life and to do the best with it, but here I feel my desires and motives need much purifying; for, even where all would sound fair enough in words, an element of self, of lurking pride, may be detected. Oh, that He would indeed purify me and make me white at any cost! No one professing to be a Christian at all could possibly have had a more cloudy, fearing, doubting, sinning, and wandering heart history than mine has been through many years.

The first part of this year (1865) I was very poorly, and on the old régime of having to give up everything, Sunday school and Saturday evening class, visiting, music, etc. It was very trying to me, specially so because I had rather built upon being stronger, and several points of interest had arisen which made me feel the more being shut off from all. But it was very good for me; I was able to feel thankful for it, and to be glad that God had taken me in hand as it were. I do not think I would have chosen otherwise than as He ordered it for me; but it seems as if my spiritual life would never go without weights, and I dread needing more discipline. [F.R.H.]

[Maria:] Deep borings, even down into darksome depths, often precede the supply of unfailing springs of refreshing water. Thus my dear sister knew much of doubt and gloom, so that she might be able to comfort others and reveal to them God's deep teachings in the darkness. Then, when she afterwards found such joy in the wells of salvation, she drew forth these teachings, refreshing other weary and thirsty ones with her words of sympathy both in poetry and prose.

---

[1] This first item is taken from *Memorials of Frances Ridley Havergal* by her sister Maria Vernon Graham Havergal (London: James Nisbet & Co., 1880), pages 72-74. It can be found on page 23 of Volume IV of Havergal's *Complete Works*. The first three paragraphs were written by F.R.H., and the last paragraph was written by her sister Maria.

[1] . . . I have never answered what you said some time back. Yes, dear, if I had my choice, I should like to be a "Christian poetess," but I do not feel I have ability enough ever to turn this line to much account. I feel as if music were a stronger talent, though in neither am I doing anything serious. Most of all would I like to be your ideal,—a winner of souls. But as no special path is open for me, I feel I can only and simply take any opportunity of using any talent which opens to me. I am not working now at composition; that door is certainly not now open, and perhaps never will be; cleverer persons than I have never been heard of; and I do not now care about getting into print, unless it should ever be made clear as my right way. I do not think of much beyond my present daily duties, teaching my nieces, etc.; or when at home, taking the various opportunities that arise of usefulness.

[2] During the winter months we opened two nice rooms every evening, and gave free invitation to young dressmakers and others, (especially those living in lodgings,) hoping that it would prove a safe and pleasant retreat for them after work hours. Classes were arranged for each evening in the smaller room; in the other, the girls read, wrote, worked, or chatted. It was not so successful as to numbers as we expected, but the attendance on the evening on which I gave a Tonic Sol-fa lesson was nearly double. I tell you frankly that it was not for the sake of Sol-fa that I began the class, but solely because I believed it was the greatest attraction I could contribute to our little scheme for bringing them within the range of Christian care and influence. My chief reason for adopting it with them, instead of the established notation, was that all the Sol-fa songs are sound and safe; and I knew I could not give them access to anything low or bad through it, while I had no such certainty had I taught the old notation. This weighed with me more than the obvious and indisputable advantages of greater facility, cheapness, etc., which the Tonic Sol-fa system has. There was no question as to the class being attractive, and great was the disappointment when, as frequently happened, the members were kept at work too late and "lost the singing."

One evening two girls came in panting and flushed, about fifteen minutes before the close. "Why, Lizzie and Jane, what *is* the matter?" "We were kept overtime! but we thought half a loaf better than no bread, so we never stopped running till we got here." They had literally run a good mile to be in time for a few minutes' singing.

---

[1] This is part of a letter F.R.H. wrote to her sister Maria in 1864. It was published in *Letters by the Late Frances Ridley Havergal* edited by her sister Maria Vernon Graham Havergal (London: James Nisbet & Co., 1885), page 33. It can be found on page 155 of Volume IV of Havergal's *Complete Works*.

[2] Frances wrote this letter in 1869 to John Spencer Curwen, the leader of the Tonic Sol-fa movement. It can be found in *Letters*, on page 165 of Volume IV of Havergal's *Complete Works*. Tonic Sol-fa is a system of music notation using letters for pitches, very different from the regular notation of notes on treble and bass clefs. John Spencer Curwen was a leader of the very prominent and successful Tonic Sol-fa movement in England.

One nice girl who had just begun forming acquaintances which would have led to no good, and to sauntering about the streets, was attracted to our rooms solely by the singing-class, but soon became one of our most regular attendants at all the classes; and we have reason to hope that she is not only saved from the dangers into which she was rushing, but that good impressions have been made, and a good work begun in her heart. I have no musical results to show, for after about eight lessons, I was interrupted by illness: but I believe that my Tonic Sol-fa class has been a grappling-iron to draw many little drifting vessels close to our side, bringing them within hearing of loving and sympathizing words, and of the One name which is sweeter than any music.

-----

[1]. . .I must tell you a wonderful bit of *Ministry of Song*, through "Whom having not seen, ye love." I was taken on speculation to call on a clever young gentleman, just an infidel, knowing the Bible and disbelieving it, and believing that nobody else really believes, but that religion is all humbug and mere profession. I was not primed at all, only knew that he was "not a religious man." In the first place, I had no end of fun with him, and got on thoroughly good terms—then was asked to sing. I prayed the whole time I was singing, and *felt* God very near and helping me. After a Handel song or two which greatly delighted him, I sang "Tell it out!" *felt* the glorious truth that He *is* King, and couldn't help breaking off in the very middle and *saying* so, right out!

Then I sang, "Whom having not seen, ye love," and felt as if I could sing out all the love of my heart in it. Well, this young infidel, who had seemed extremely surprised and subdued by "Tell it out," competely broke down, and went away to hide his tears in a bay window. And afterwards we sat down together, and he let me "tell it out" as I pleased, and it was not hard to speak of Him of whom I had sung. He seemed altogether struck and subdued, and listened like a child. He said, "Well there *is* faith then, *you* have it anyhow—I saw it when you sang, and I could not stand it, and that's the fact!" He was anxious for me to come again.

When I came away, his sister, who had introduced me, wept for joy, saying she had persuaded me to come with a vague hope that he " *might* find he could tolerate a religious person," but never dared to hope such an effect as this, and that she thought I had been most marvellously guided in drawing the bow at a venture, for every word and even action had been just right. I tell you this just because you are publishing both "Tell it out" and other leaflets for me. Will you sometimes pray that God's especial blessing will go with them? I should add that it was almost a miracle in another way, for I had such a wretched cold that I doubted being able to sing *at all,* and yet I believe I never sang clearer and better and stronger. How *good* God is!

-----

[1] F.R.H. was a wonderfully gifted pianist, and she accompanied herself on the piano. This is part of a letter to James Parlane in 1876, found in *Letters*, on pages 221-222 of Volume IV of Havergal's *Complete Works*.

[1]My dear sister Frances went to Swansea on Thursday, 17th. I sent our good maid M. Farrington with her, as she did not wish me to go; she says that on the way Miss Frances talked so humbly, and that she "felt as if she had no right to go teaching others—such a sinner as I am; but then Mary, I am just trusting for every word." The room was quite full. Mrs. Morgan, not knowing F.'s subject, had chosen a hymn that did not suit it, and my sister always thought it important that hymns should be suitably chosen. As her subject for the evening was from Hosea 3, "I also for thee," (See *Starlight through the Shadows*), F. said she wished to sing "Precious Saviour, may I live, only for Thee." Mrs. Morgan said they did not know her tune to it ("Onesimus," *S. G. G.* 257.) F.: "No fear! Do let me just sing one verse alone, and I know they will join." Going to the piano and turning her face to them, she sang with her own bright ringing cheeriness one verse, and then all joined most heartily with her. Mary told me of my sister's soft pleading voice—that her words were intensely tender and entreating. At the close of the meeting, my sister gave to each one a card with her Consecration hymn, "Take my life and let it be Consecrated, Lord, to Thee," specially prepared and printed for this evening (Messrs. Parlane, Paisley, still supply them). Her own name was omitted, and a blank space left for signature. As she gave the cards, she asked them to make that hymn a test before God, and if they could really do so, to sign it on their knees at home. Then the hymn was sung to our dear father's tune "Patmos" (No. 145, *S. G. G.*).

It seems to have been a great night of decision to many present. The next morning, before ever her breakfast was finished, one and another came for conversation with my dear sister—a French governess was specially impressed. My sister returned very much exhausted—meetings seemed to take away her little physical strength, and yet she always cheerfully took up any work for her King.

CONSECRATION HYMN.

'Here we offer and present unto Thee, O Lord, ourselves, our souls and bodies, to be a reasonable, holy, and lively sacrifice unto Thee.'

TAKE my life, and let it be
Consecrated, Lord, to Thee.

Take my moments and my days;
Let them flow in ceaseless praise.

Take my hands, and let them move
At the impulse of Thy love.

Take my feet, and let them be
Swift and 'beautiful' for Thee.

Take my voice, and let me sing
Always, only, for my King.

---

[1] Her sister Maria wrote this next account of two paragraphs—a "Memorandum by M.V.G.H."—in her edition of Frances' *Letters*. It can be found on page 238 of Volume IV of Havergal's *Complete Works*.

Take my lips, and let them be
Filled with messages from Thee.

Take my silver and my gold;
Not a mite would I withhold.

Take my intellect, and use
Every power as Thou shalt choose.

Take my will, and make it Thine;
It shall be no longer mine.

Take my heart, it *is* Thine own;
It shall be Thy royal throne.

Take my love; my Lord, I pour
At Thy feet its treasure-store.

Take myself, and I will be
Ever, *only*, ALL for Thee.

---

[1] I well remember when Frances first thought of writing "My King." We were returning from Switzerland. Her illness there had quite hindered any writing, and she seemed to regret having no book ready for Christmas. It was October 21st, we had passed Oxford station, on our way to Winterdyne, and I thought she was dozing, when she exclaimed, with that herald flash in her eye, "Marie! I see it all, I can write a little book, 'My King'" and rapidly went through divisions for thirty-one chapters. The setting sun shone on her face; and, even then, it seemed to me she could not be far distant from the land of the King. Illness came on again, accompanied by severe suffering, yet the book was quickly written and published.

---

[2] Perhaps you would hardly guess how very much what you said about *My King* delighted and encouraged me. I never expected *men* to read or care for it,—I did not aim higher than girls of whom I have a considerable following. It is far more than I hoped,—for I am not one of those terrible "strong-minded women," but I think we have quite "rights" enough in proportion to our powers and position. And I never thought of reaching *men* by anything I might write; yet you and others are willing to listen to the little things I have to say, and I take it as an extra token for good—the more pleasant, because unsought and unexpected. I am following it up with two new books (now nearly finished printing), *Royal Commandments* and *Royal Bounty.* I am inclined to envy your

---

[1] Frances' sister Maria V. G. Havergal wrote this in her biography *Memorials of Frances Ridley Havergal.* It can be found on page 58 of Volume IV of Havergal's *Complete Works.*
[2] This is part of a letter she wrote to Samuel Gillespie Prout, 1877. Prout had written the book *Never Say Die,* ending with his poem "Loving all along." This book was so valuable to F.R.H., who had edited it and prepared it for publication. She also set the poem to music. The whole book can be found in Volume II of Havergal's *Complete Works.* This letter to Prout can be found in *Letters,* on page 226 of Volume IV of the *Complete Works.*

special gift of heart-words to the *very* far off—it seems so much more like the Master than mine; but still it is very sweet to be allowed to write for our fellow-servants, which is what I most often seem led to do.

---

[1]January 25, 1878.

I meant to have set to work this morning at my new book, *The Royal Invitation,* but instead of that, I give the time to *prayer,* and requests for prayer about it. *To-morrow* I hope to begin.

Now I ask you most earnestly to pray about it, and to pass on the request to any other friends who, though unknown personally, will kindly do me this GREATEST service of "helping together by prayer." I never felt such need of it. The thing is so on my mind, that I can better understand than ever before, what the old prophets meant by "the burden of the Lord." I must write it—I must set aside other things for it; and yet, most strangely, I have not two ideas as to *what* to say! all I know is that the title must be *The Royal Invitation,* and the keynote must be "COME!" I can't see beyond that! But I entirely expect that when I sit down to-morrow, the Lord will give me what He means me to say.

You see, I have only written for Christians as yet (with the exception of a few leaflets), and so I have not fulfilled the great commission, "Let him that heareth, say, *Come,*" in writing, though of course I am often at it in speaking. So *now* I want to peal out a "COME!" that shall be *heard* and followed; a "Come!" especially to those who are not reached by tracts or little books in paper covers, but who would not reject a pretty gift-book of daily readings, not too long and not too prosy.

It will want special tact and power, and all that I have *not* got, and must therefore look only to the Lord for! The other books have opened a wide door for it; and if I am enabled to do it at all, it will probably go by *tens of thousands,* and so it is an immense responsibility to dare to write it. I feel as if it were hardly less than preaching to one of Moody's enormous congregations!

Now won't you and your good friends help me mightily about it? Ask that He would give me EVERY SINGLE WORD from beginning to end, that I may leave *nothing* unsaid which should be said, and not say one word which is not really from Him. One may as well ask much as little, while one *is* about it! So please ask that it may be FULL OF POWER—that every chapter may be a channel of converting grace—that it may be more really and definitely blessed to souls than anything I have yet written—that it may be a sort of condensed Mission Week to every reader. Have you faith enough to ask all that? . . .

There! Have I asked too much? I don't mean of the Lord, but of you? What, if this time next year, I am writing to ask you for help in praise for an immense answer? WE SHALL SEE.

—Yours in our dear Master.

---

[1] The next three items are excerpts from letters that Frances wrote just before and as she wrote *The Royal Invitation.* They can be found in *Letters by the Late Frances Ridley Havergal,* on pages 258-259 and 228-229 of Volume IV of Havergal's *Complete Works.*

(*To Leonard Bickerstaff.*)

February 7, 1878.

I have a request to you, for which yours to me gives opportunity. Will you take it up as a little bit of special praying work during the next few days? I have written twenty-two chapters of my new book, *The Royal Invitation; or, Daily Thoughts on coming to Christ,* and I do long for very special help for the nine chapters which remain to be written. I want the Lord to give me every word, and not let me write a word without Him, nor a sentence that is not a message from Him. I do so want to win those who have never yet come to Jesus. Will you ask this for me every day till about next Thursday, by which day I shall about finish, please God.

Why not join both the Scripture-reading Unions? Ever so many are members of both. Both are good solid bread, but I prefer the whole loaf to the half one, both for myself, and more especially for the sake of the many whom I thus induce to read twice a day, who otherwise would read only once. I have often said to others, "Join Mr. Richardson's Union for the sake of your personal friends, but join Mr. Boys' for the sake of work among others." The one chapter a day is a pleasant *link,* but the two chapters are a *lever* to raise those who need raising to fuller feeding on the Word. I myself have joined both.

—Yours affectionately in our dear Master.

February 14, 1878.

The twelve o'clock prayer to-day was commuted into thanksgiving for completed work; so I write at once to tell you that the good Lord has given it me all, and fully answered the prayer that it might be done without difficulty or strain. I have now merely to put it straight for the press, fill in the references, and send it off. But the last sentence is written! I shall write no preface; the title is, *The Royal Invitation; or, Daily Thoughts on Coming to Christ,* and I prefer leaving it to the reader to find out who I am aiming at.

I shall next see about a re-cast of the *Ministry of Song,* and *Under the Surface* for one volume, *Life Mosaic.* This will be an opportunity of dropping out a dozen or two of the weakest pieces, and I must ask clear guidance to do this judiciously. Next, I want to arrange *Daily Melodies for the King's Minstrels.* I am reserving MS. poems for a still future book.

---

[1]The first opportunity I had, I only approached the subject sideways with ——. He probably saw what I was at, for he sheered off so very quickly and

---

[1] This was taken from *Letters,* on pages 192-193 of Volume IV of Havergal's *Complete Works.* The first excerpt shows how she truly loved lost people the same as if that were herself lost in sins and at the edge of hell, a true example of the two commandments (Matt. 22:37-40). Her conversation with the man recorded in this letter shows the fervency of her love for unbelievers. The second excerpt shows how F.R.H. is reminiscent of a statement by John Newton: "I endeavour to keep all Shibboleths, and forms and terms of distinction out of sight, as we keep knives and razors out of the way of children, and if my hearers had not other means of information, I think they would not know from me that there are such creatures as Arminians or Calvinists in the world. But we talk a good deal about Christ." (from *John Newton A Biography*

pointedly to another topic, that I thought it best not to renew the attack, but adopt different tactics next time. So then I made a full front attack, which gave *no* chance of evasion, telling him straight out my fears and hopes and prayers for him personally. He staid nearly an hour! arguing, cavilling, and twisting about like an eel. He manœuvred ingeniously to get me off Bible-ground, and entangle me in metaphysical thickets, but I know one is never safe but in standing firm on the Word and declining to use Saul's weapons—so he always found himself confronted with a smooth stone out of the brook, and thereby brought back again and again to personalities—"And what about his own soul and salvation?" But I saw no *impression;* so far I have only delivered my own soul.[1] I think I was, however, enabled to speak winningly to him, and that he was a little touched by the reality of my anxiety for his salvation. He will be a real trophy for Jesus if converted, perhaps almost more so than any one in ——. I was so exhausted after it, that I only had three-quarters of an hour's sleep the whole night, having got quite overwrought.

———

There is infinitely *more* involved in this than you seem to have the least idea of. And nothing but God's own power can teach it you. It is true my attention was called to this truth, and that set me thinking and praying (at first it was kicking!). No human word did or could open my eyes—it all came clear to me in one tremendous flash, one Sunday at Perry, when I was quite alone. I have no doubt it was the Spirit himself revealing it, even by the effects, for it is since then that all has been so different. Now will you only let your mind be open to receive *whatever* teaching He may send you? (I do not mean any words of mine). I repeat, *no* human argument can do anything, but rather making one kick the more "against the pricks." Will you for this one week, really pray that He would guide you into His own truth *whatever* that may be, and that you may be made *willing* to give up *any* "opinion" which is *not* His truth. The importance of it lies here—as long as you do not attribute all your salvation to God, so long you are defrauding Him of the glory which is His due. Who hath made you to differ? *Why* do you believe and rest in Jesus when others do not? *Is that difference your doing or His?* Could you have come to Jesus if He had not drawn you? And if He did draw you, why *you* and not everybody? If you are indeed "beloved" now, *when* did He begin to love you?

One *or* other made the choice in the first place, either *you* or *God.* If *you* did, then *you* had a share in saving yourself, and it all hinged upon your doing or not doing. If *He* did, then why deny Him the praise and thanksgiving for having

by Bernard Martin, London: William Heinemann, Ltd., 1950, page 275). In all of Havergal's Complete Works, not one instance has been found where she used the word "Calvinist" or the word "reformed," although to a person who well understands F.R.H., there is little or no question that she understood and believed reformed doctrine. The First Day of *My King* is one of many examples that show clearly what she knew, believed, and loved. She believed and loved the "doctrines of grace," yet she never participated in divisive partisanship. So, F.R.H. worked passionately for the salvation of souls, and yet she firmly believed that conversion was the sovereign work of God alone.

[1] This is likely referring to Ezekiel 33:1-9.

chosen *you,* even you! O give glory to the Lord your God, yes, *all* the glory. At present, though you do not know it, you *are* defrauding Him of praise.

Words are often terrible hindrances, "darkening counsel,"—such is your word "favouritism"; say "sovereignty" instead—absolute, but *righteous,* though inscrutable—and then *bow* to it, and you will end by rejoicing in it. Besides you only shift the difficulty, for whose doing is it that one is born in England and another among the darkness and cruelty of Timbuctoo? *God* chose to give you English birth and Christian training, and has utterly denied the same great advantages to others. You *must* call this favouritism if anything is—I call it sovereignty. Give up that "vain word," and you will see clearer. I have been running through a Gospel of St. John for you, only because I could not find a Romans, Ephesians, or Thessalonians portion, which I should have taken in preference as to *strength* of argument. Will you accede to this most earnest request—that you will read this Gospel, *i.e.* the first seventeen chapters, prayerfully through—*willing* to receive *His* truth at *any* cost or sacrifice of "opinion" or "theory" or "idea."[1] Oh, do not glance at it lightly, I am very anxious that you should not do so. I cannot explain all you will gain by receiving His truth as a little child; but I know it because I have felt and found it so. And will you make it a great subject of REAL prayer for light and teaching? I believe that in such things, John 7:17: "If any man will do His will, he shall know of the doctrine whether it be of God," is signally fulfilled, if we are made *quite* willing to give up our own will about theories and ideas and to follow His teaching, even if quite contrary to what we fancied or liked; then He lets us "*know* of the doctrine whether it be of God." It lies at the very root of ever so many other difficulties; but once receive it, and all falls into place, while the spiritual "strong meat" *does* strengthen in a way I would not and could not have believed till His own Hand fed me with it. . . . Have you ever noticed the preposition in Revelation 5:9? I shall never forget how breathlessly I turned to the Greek, *hoping* it was wrongly translated, and found it was even *more* emphatic in the original: "Hast redeemed us to God by Thy blood *out* of every kindred, and tongue, and people, and nation." I most fully agree with you in all you say as to the lost. It will be their own fault, and they will own the *justice,* and yet the salvation of the saved will be *all* God's glory and His doing *from beginning to end.* I do not care to reconcile the paradox—both are true and revealed—the day shall declare it. This is one of the points I want you to be clear upon. Upon *what* does your *actual* salvation (not your *possible* salvation) depend? Is *the* hinge your faith? or is it *God's* sovereign and free gift to you *personally* of it? *i.e.* of the faith as well as the grace. If the former, you must have the credit of making the difference between yourself and others, and not God. Yes, dear,—that is just what I want, not argument, but the Holy Spirit's light and help—coming closer. Let us both seek that.

---

[1] Frances apparently took an individual copy of John's Gospel, not having an individual copy of other books at hand (no photocopiers in that day, though copies of John were printed for ones to give freely), and marked specific verses in the copy of John for this one to read.

[1]…"I have not been able to communicate with any publisher till a few days ago, since October, when I gave the MS. of *Little Pillows* and *Morning Bells* to Nisbet. Well, we boldly started an edition of 4000 each! which were *not* in time for the advantage of Christmas orders. Yet in seven weeks we had to reprint them! Also, they are going to be translated and published by the Religious Tract Society of France; and also some one in high places is going to give them to all the royal children. Caswell had to reprint my *Five Benefits* four times in as many weeks, the demand was so great! The same principle holds, does it not, dear J., in everything (I do not mean but that we are to do our very best when able)—the more entirely a burden, a care, or a work is cast on the Lord, the more entirely He *takes* it for us. It is so restful to have given up altogether to Him body, soul, and spirit—all one has and is—unreservedly. Life is a different thing thenceforth."

---

[2]May 1879.

I will tell you the *worst* first! It's all up about Mr. Sankey singing "Loving all along" in England. He has asthma or something worse; is forbidden to sing at all; is giving up all his engagements here, and going back to America next month. So he only tinkles on the piano. Then the very day he came, I started a feverish attack which threatened to get serious, but mercifully is diminishing this morning; but when I shall be able to sing again I don't know! as I am in bed of course. However, I did sing "Loving all along" directly he came, as I knew I might get no other chance, though it was a poor chance enough to sing it with a splitting headache and an icy chill down my spine. And the first thing Sankey said was that "it wouldn't do for America at all"! because, "Tramp, tramp" is their most popular war song, and it would never do for him to sing it!

Now for the other side.

Next morning he said, "That song of yours abides with me, that *big one!* I woke up with it. There's two or three points that *haunt* me." "That's all right," said I, "for *I* woke up with a way out of the American difficulty. 'Far, far on the downward way,' etc., instead of 'Tramp,' if the author does not object." Then he looked very serious (which he generally does not), and said, "It's my belief that song has *got* to *go*. And that *I'll have* to sing it! It's kind of taken a *hold* of me"! So then we looked carefully through the song, for as I have not heard him sing, I could not tell if it would suit his voice, and was ready to alter and carve as much as he liked, but oh, dear no, he would not have a single note touched. I was "*just to go right ahead,*" and write it out for press, exactly as it stood.

---

[1] This was part of a letter that F.R.H. wrote to Julia Kirchhoffer in 1876, found in *Letters*, on page 216 of Volume IV of Havergal's *Complete Works*. Julia Georgianna Mary Kirchhoffer (1855-1876) was the author of *Poems and Essays*, for which F.R.H. wrote a preface. This book was posthumously published by Frances' friends J. & R. Parlane, very possibly because of her advocacy. Frances had an exceptionally high regard for her works, and her letters to Julia are so full of good advice, friendship, and love.

[2] She wrote this letter to Samuel Gillespie Prout. This was one of her last letters, written in May before she died June 3, 1879, found in *Letters*, on page 239 of Volume IV.

I hope you won't feel it needful to give thanks *under protest* for the answer to your prayer under protest! The Baroness von Cramm is extremely struck with the music, which she says is "so dramatic and so beautiful," and I know you won't be sorry to hear this! All the same, I do not think the song will be popular, because it is just one of those which is utterly ruined if stumbled over, or even if well played by one who does not DASH off the recitative-like style with real *spirit,* and bring out the *sharp* contrasts which give effect. But if nobody else *ever* sings it but Sankey and the Baroness in their different spheres, those two are worth thousands of ordinary singers, and if not a copy sells, the two copies that go to them, may do more real work for God than a dozen editions. So we will *thank God* and take courage. Besides, though I cannot sing like them, I know I can make some listen to *"Loving—*ALL *along*!*"* and perhaps God will give *me* a little fruit thereby besides what they will get.

I go off to Ireland on my mission station tour on June 4 (*D.V.*). Have been "marvellously helped" in total abstinence work here, and got 120 to sign in this little village of Newton—at least, chiefly in the village and a few around—mostly children, but it is spreading upwards. I am quite astonished at what God has wrought. I never dreamt of asking for so many as He has given me for my "Newton Temperance."

"HOW WONDERFUL!"

HE answered all my prayer abundantly,
    And crowned the work that to His feet I brought,
    With blessing more than I had asked or thought—
A blessing undisguised, and fair, and free.
I stood amazed, and whispered, "Can it be
    That He hath granted all the boon I sought?
    How wonderful that He for me hath wrought!
How wonderful that He hath answered me!"
O faithless heart! He *said* that He would hear
    And answer Thy poor prayer, and He *hath* heard
And proved His promise. Wherefore didst thou fear?
    Why marvel that Thy Lord hath kept His word?
More wonderful if He should fail to bless
Expectant faith and prayer with good success!

Frances Ridley Havergal
August 30, 1873 at Oakhampton

III. PROSE PIECES

[1]ONE HOUR WITH JESUS.

"What! could ye not watch with Me one hour?"

An echo of this utterance of pathetic surprise, this wonderfully gentle reproof, seems to float around a matter of daily experience, and, with too many, of daily faithlessness. Our Divine Master has called us to no Gethsemane-watch of strange and mysterious darkness. It is while the brightness of day is breaking—perhaps even long after it has broken—that His call to communion with Himself reaches our not always willing ear. "Come with me!" (Song of Solomon 4:8). And the drowsy reply too often is, "Presently, Lord! not just this minute!"

And then, after "yet a little sleep, a little slumber, a little folding of the hands to sleep," the precious hour is past which "might have been" so full of blessing.

"What! could ye not watch with Me one hour?"

What is the practical answer of very many of His disciples?

"Oh, *yes!* very easily and readily, when the 'one hour' is at night, and we do not feel particularly inclined to go to bed, especially if we have a nice fire to 'watch' by. But oh, *no!* if the 'one hour' involves getting up at seven instead of eight, especially on a cold and gloomy morning. *That* is a very different matter!"

Were the question asked, "What one thing do you suppose has most hindered the largest number of Christians this day and this year in their spiritual life and growth?" I should reply unhesitatingly, "Probably the temptation not to rise in time to put on their armour as well as their dress before breakfast."

A mere ten minutes—is that enough preparation for our warfare and provision for our wants; for spreading all our needs and difficulties before the Lord; for telling Jesus all that is in our hearts; for bringing before Him all the details of our work; for searching to know His mind and His will; for storing His word in our hearts; for replenishing our seed-baskets, that we may have something to sow, and getting Him to sharpen our sickles that we may reap; for confession and supplication and intercession, and, above all, for *praise?*

Ten minutes or a quarter of an hour! Is that enough for the many things which He has to say unto us? for the quiet teachings of His Spirit, for the dawning of His light on the dark sayings of old, and the flashing of His glory and power on the words which are spirit and life? Is that enough to spend in converse with the Friend of friends? Does this look as if we really cared very much about Him? Even if it were enough for our small, cool affection, is it enough, think you, for His great love? enough to satisfy the Heart that is waiting to commune with ours? He loves us so much that He will have us with

---

[1] "One Hour with Jesus" is a truthful, beautiful, compassionate entreaty to believers to spend one hour at the start of each day alone with the Lord, reading His Word and praying to Him. Originally published as a pamphlet, this is found on pages 3-9 of Volume II of Havergal's *Complete Works*.

Him forever, and we love Him so little that we did not care to turn out of bed this morning in time to have even half-an-hour of real intercourse with Him. For it would have been "with Him." There was no doubt about His being at the tryst. He slumbered not; "He faileth not"—but we failed. What have we missed this morning! How do we know what He may have had to say to us? What have we missed all the mornings of this past year!

"But it comes to the same thing if I go up-stairs after breakfast!" *Does* it "come to the same thing"? You know perfectly, and by repeated experience, that it *does not*. Letters and newspapers have come; you stay to read them, you must just see what So-and-so says, and what the telegrams are; and then you must just attend to sundry little duties, and then somebody wants you, and then you really ought to go out, and so perhaps you never "go up-stairs" at all. Or, if you do, perhaps your room is not "done," or you are interrupted or called down. Satan is astonishingly ingenious in defeating these good after-breakfast intentions. And yet these external devices are not his strongest. Suppose you do get away after breakfast without external hindrance or interruption, he has other moves to make. Do you not find that the "things which are seen" have got the start of the "things which are not seen"? not necessarily sinful things, but simply the "*other* things entering in" which are "not the things which are Jesus Christ's," yet they choke the word, and hinder prayer. You have an unsettled feeling; you do not feel sure you will not be wanted or interrupted; it is an effort—pretty often an unsuccessful one—to forget the news, public or private, which has come by post; bits of breakfast table-talk come back to mind; voices or sounds in the now stirring household distract you; you ought, you know you ought, to be doing something else at that hour, unless, indeed, you are a drone in the home-hive, or willfully "out of work" as to the Lord's vineyard. And so it does *not* "come to the same thing" at all, but you go forth ungirded to the race, unarmed to the warfare. What marvel if faintness and failure are the order of the day!

I suppose there is not one of us who has not made "good resolutions" about this, and—broken them. And this is not very surprising, considering that "good resolutions" are never mentioned in the Bible as any item of armour or weapons for "the good fight of faith." So let us try something better.

First, *Purpose.* This is what we want; neither languid and lazy wishing, nor fitful and impulsive resolving, but calm and humble and steady purpose, like David's (Psalm 17:3), Daniel's (Daniel 1:8), and St. Paul's (2 Timothy 3:10). Without purpose, even prayer is paralyzed, and answer prevented. Now, have we any purpose in this matter? in other words, do we really *mean* to do what we say we wish to do? If not, let us ask at once that the grace of purpose may be wrought in us by the Spirit of all grace.

Secondly, *Prayer.* Having purposed by His grace, let us ask that our purpose may, also by His grace, be carried into effect. It will not do merely to lament and pray vaguely about it. To-morrow morning will not do; the thing must be done to-night. To-night, then, tell the gracious Master all about it, tell Him of the past disloyalty and sin in this matter, so that you may go to the coming battle strong in the strength of His pardoning love and His cleansing blood, and

His tenderly powerful "Go, and sin no more." Do not make a good resolution about all the mornings of your life—His way is "morning by morning" (Isaiah 50:4), and His way is best. Ask Him to give you the grace of energy for this one coming morning, if you are spared to see it. Ask Him to give you a holy night, that you may remember Him upon your bed, and that even the half-conscious moments may be full of Him. Ask Him that when you awake you may be "still with Him," and that He would then enable you unreluctantly to rise, eager and glad to watch with Him "one hour," uninterrupted and quiet, "alone with Jesus."

Even Prayer and Purpose may be neutralized by want of—

Thirdly, *Self-denying Forethought.* We almost make the difficulty for ourselves when we forget that we can not burn a candle at both ends. If we *will* sit up at night, of course we make it harder in proportion to get up in the morning. "I would give anything to be able to get this precious 'one hour'!" says a lie-a-bed Christian, or one who really needs a long night's sleep. No! there is one thing you will not give for it, and that is an hour of your pleasant evenings. It is too much to expect you to leave the cosy fireside, or the delightful book, or the lively circle an hour earlier, so that you may go to bed in good time, and be more ready to rise in the morning. No; you could not really be expected to include *that* in the "anything" you are ready to give for the true "early communion" with your Lord. And yet only try it, and see if the blessing is not a hundredfold more than the little sacrifice.

Perhaps we hardly need say that the habit of reading any ordinary book after we go up-stairs, "only just a few pages, you know," is simply fatal to the sweet and sacred "one hour," whether that night or next morning. Oh, let your own room at any rate be sacred to the One Blessed Guest! Do not keep Him waiting, because you "wanted just to finish a chapter" of any book but His own. Finishing one chapter too often leads to beginning another, and to filling the mind with "other things." And then, "Dear me, I had no idea it was so late!" And, all the while, the King was waiting! What wonder that you find the audience chamber closed, when you at last put down your book!

Will not this be enough? Not quite. Not even Purpose and Prayer and Self-denying Forethought are enough without—

Fourthly, *Trust.* Here is the joint in the harness, the breaking-down point. Praying, and not trusting Him to answer; putting on other pieces of armour, and not covering them all with the shield of faith; asking Him to do something for us, and then not entrusting ourselves to Him to have it done for us. Distrusting one's self is one thing; distrusting Jesus is quite another. No matter at all, nay, so much the better that you feel, "I have failed morning after morning; I am at my wits' end; I can not summon resolution, when the moment comes, to jump up; it is no use making resolutions, I only break them again and again!" Only, do not stop there. "I *can't*, but Jesus *can!*" will settle this, and everything else.

"I *can't* make myself get up, therefore—*i.e.*, just *because* I can't—I will put it into my Lord's hands, and trust Him to make me get up. He will undertake for me even in this." One feels humbled and ashamed to be reduced to this, and rightly enough; it proves how despicably weak we are. The apparent smallness of the trial enhances the greatness of the failure. It adds new force to "Without Me ye can do nothing," when conscience whispers, "Exactly so! nothing! not even get out of bed at the right moment!"

But it is when we have come to this point, and see that all the strength of ourselves and our resolutions *is* utter weakness, that we see there is nothing for it but to say, "Jesus, I will trust *Thee!*" Say that to Him to-night with reference to this often lost battle. Trust, simply and really *trust,* Him to win it for you, and you will see that He will not disappoint your trust. He NEVER does! The secret of success is trust in Him who "faileth not," and learning this secret in this one thing, may and should lead you to trust, and therefore to succeed, in many another battle. For—

> "From victory to victory
> His army shall be led."

But what about His suffering ones, His physically weak ones, who can not or must not rise early? How glad we are that the true reason or motive is "opened unto the eyes of Him with whom we have to do," the High-Priest who is "touched with the feeling of our infirmities!" He knows these cases, and, "in some way or other, the Lord will provide"; His grace will be sufficient, and that which is spiritual loss, if arising from our own indolence, will be turned into spiritual gain if arising from His accepted chastening. I think our dear Master will see to it that these shall not be losers; He will give opportunity, and grace to take it; He can even give quietness and communion amid the mid-day surroundings. Still, unquestionably, special watchfulness and special grace are needed, when, through ill-health, the usual early hour can not be secured.

These may surely take all the comfort of His most gracious words, "The spirit indeed is willing, but the flesh is weak." They are never to be perverted into excuse for sinful indolence; and it is never to be allowed that our Lord could have spoken excusingly of that flesh figurative, which is to be crucified, mortified, reckoned dead, given no quarter whatever. But they are gracious indeed, as referring to this literal mortal flesh in which the life of Jesus is to be made manifest, the body of which He is the Saviour, the frame which He tenderly "remembereth." Many a mistake arises from confusing these two distinct meanings of the word.

Some who are not invalids, have yet great difficulties, owing to household arrangements over which they have no control. Since these thoughts were first printed, I have received so many touching letters from younger or dependent members of Christian households, that I can not refuse to insert a loving appeal to my senior friends not to hinder any under their roofs in this most important matter. A late or uncertain hour for evening prayers is a more serious hindrance to young or delicate persons, or those who have had a busy day, than they imagine. "They do not like me to leave the room before prayers; and afterwards I am so tired that I really *can't* enjoy my Bible as I wish." If "*they*" only knew how the stereotyped domestic arrangements are hindering the grace of God in the heart of daughter, visitor, governess, or servant, surely, oh, surely! it would not be thought too great a sacrifice to "have prayers a little earlier." At *least,* no hindrance by word, or even look, should be placed in the way of any one's slipping away earlier in the evening, for a little time alone with Him *before* they are "too tired," and returning when the bell rings for family worship. Then retiring *immediately* to rest, the inestimable "one hour" in the morning need not be lost through physical weariness which a little kind consideration might avoid. In this matter—

> Evil is wrought by want of thought,
> As well as want of heart.

Let us not forget, but remember in grateful contrast, how many there are who have to be hard at work before our earliest thoughts of rising; to whom "an hour earlier" would be a physical impossibility, the long day's work being followed by unpeaceful evenings in the noisy dwellings of noisy alleys. No quiet for them till long after we are in our quiet rooms; the short interval between the latest sounds of drunkenness and the inexorable factory-bell being perhaps still further shortened by a long distance to walk. And no quiet corner to retire to, no possibility of kneeling "*alone* with Jesus," at any time of day or night! Will not some who thus have to seek Him "in the press," rise up in judgment against us who may have an undisturbed hour alone with Him every morning, if we will?

The following testimony is from one of England's most successful and eminent men of business. He writes:—

"In the busy life I have lived, I owe much to the practice of very early rising to secure the 'hour with Jesus' which you recommend. Even now, I find very early rising essential to the maintenance of spiritual life and close communion with God; and being now somewhat weak physically, nothing but the *desire* for this communion is sufficient to enable me to rise.

"My wife rises about 6, remaining in her room till 8, or she would not, with her large household, be equal, spiritually, to her duties."

Is not this one of the many "new leaves" which onward-pressing pilgrims should desire to turn over with the New Year? And will it not be the truest means of ensuring a Happy New Year? Happier, brighter, holier, more useful and more victorious; more radiant with His Presence and more full of His Power than any previous one.

The time past of our lives may surely suffice us for the neglect of this entirely personal and entirely precious privilege. We have suffered loss enough;—shall we not henceforth, "from this time," seek the gain, the spiritual wealth which this "one hour" will assuredly bring? Cold mornings! well, the good Master who knoweth our frame and its natural shrinking from "His cold" knows all about them. But was there ever an added difficulty for which He could not and would not give added strength and "more grace"? So do not let us wait for the summer mornings which may never be ours to spend in earthly communion, nor even for the childish idea of making a special start on NEW YEAR'S DAY.

When we are "called" *to-morrow* morning, let it remind us of her who "called Mary her sister, saying, The Master is come, and calleth for thee." For He will certainly be there, waiting for us. What will you do? We know what Mary did. "*As soon as* she heard that, she arose quickly, and came unto Him."

¹THE SOURCE OF THE KINGSHIP.

"Because the Lord hath loved His people, He hath made thee king over them."
—2 CHRONICLES 2:11; 9:8.

Christ said to His Father, "Thou lovedst me before the foundation of the world." At that mysterious date, not of time, but of everlasting love, God "chose us in Him." Before the world began, God, that cannot lie, gave the promise of eternal life to Him for us, and made with Him for us "a covenant ordered in all things, and sure." The leading provisions of that covenant were, a Lamb for our atonement, and a King for our government—a dying and a living Saviour. This God the Father did for us, and His own divine interest is strongly indicated in the typical words, "God will provide *Himself* a Lamb," and "I have provided *me* a King." So the Source of the Kingship of Christ is God Himself, in the eternal counsels of His love. It is one of the grand "thoughts of God." *(John 17:24; Ephesians 1:4; Titus 1:2; 2 Samuel 23:5; Genesis 22:8; 1 Samuel 16:1; Psalm 139:17)*

Having provided, He appointed and anointed His King: "Yet have I set (margin, anointed) my King upon my holy hill of Zion." What a marvellous meeting-place is thus found in the Kingship of Jesus for God's heart and ours! He says in His majestic sovereignty, "I have set *my* King"; and we say in lowly and loving loyalty, "Thou art *my* King." *(Psalm 2:6; Psalm 44:4)*

God has appointed His King "to be ruler over Israel *and* over Judah." Thus He gives his children a great bond of union. For "one King shall be King to them all," and He shall "gather together in one the children of God which were scattered abroad." "Satan scatters, but Jesus gathers." Shall we then let the enemy have his way, and induce us to keep apart and aloof from those over whom our beloved King reigns also? Let us try this day to recollect this, and make it practical in all our contact with His other subjects. *(1 Kings 1:35; Ezekiel 37:22; John 11:52)*

Why has God made Jesus King? Who would have guessed the right answer? "*Because* the Lord loved His people." So the very thought of the Kingship of Christ sprang from the everlasting love of God to His people. Bring that wonderful statement down to personal reality,—"His people," that is, *you and me.* God made Jesus King over you, because He loved you, and that with nothing less than the love wherewith He loved Him. Which is the more wonderful—the love that devised such a gift, or the gift that was devised by such love! Oh, to realize the glorious value of it! May we, who by His grace know something of God's gift of His Son as our Saviour, learn day by day more of the magnificent preciousness of His gift of His Anointed One as our King! *(Jeremiah 31:3; John 17:26)*

---

¹ This is the "First Day" of the 31-day book *My King.*

[1]THE INDWELLING OF THE KING.

"Is not her King in her?"—JEREMIAH 8:19.

Waiting for a royal coming,—what expectation, what preparation, what tension! A glimpse for many, a full view for some, a word for a favoured few, and the pageant is over like a dream. The Sovereign may come, but does not stay.

Our King comes not thus: He comes not to pass, but to "*dwell* in the midst of thee"; not only in His Church collectively, but in each believer individually. We pray, "Abide with us," and He answers in the sublime plural of Godhead, "We will come unto him and make our abode with him." Even this grand abiding with us does not extend to the full marvels of His condescension and His nearness, for the next time He speaks of it He changes the "with" to "in," and thenceforth only speaks of "I *in* you," "I in him," "I in them." — Zechariah 2:10 / 2 Cor. 6:16 / Luke 24:29 / John 14:23 / John 15:4, 5 / John 17:23

Now do not let us say, "How can this be?" but, like Mary, "How shall this be?" The means, though not the mode, of the mystery is revealed for our grasp of adoring wonder: "That Christ may dwell in your heart by faith." It is almost too wonderful to dare to speak of. Christ Himself, my King, coming to me, into me! abiding, dwelling in my very heart! Really staying there all day, all night, wherever I am, whatever I am doing; here in my poor unworthy heart at this very moment! And this only because the grace that flowed from His own love has broken the bars of doubt, and because He has given the faith that wanted Him and welcomed Him. Let us pause a little to take it in! — John 3:9 / Luke 1:34 / Ephesians 3:17 / Jeremiah 31:3 / Ephesians 2:8

The more we have known of the plague of our own heart, the more inconceivably wonderful this indwelling of Christ will appear,—much more wonderful than that He chose a manger as His royal resting-place, for that had never been defiled by sin, and had never harboured His enemy. It is no use trying to comprehend this incomprehensible grace of our King,—we have only to believe His promise, saying, "Amen; the Lord God of my Lord the King say so too." — 1 Kings 8:38 / Luke 2:7 / 1 Kings 1:36

There should be three practical results of this belief:—1. *Holiness.* We must see to it that we resolutely "put away" all that ought not to be in His royal abode. "Having, therefore, these promises, dearly beloved, let us cleanse ourselves from *all* filthiness of the flesh and spirit, perfecting holiness in the fear of God." 2. *Confidence.* What does the citadel fear when an invincible general is within it? "The Lord thy God in the midst of thee is mighty; He will save." — Ephesians 4:31 / 1 Cor. 3:16, 17 / 2 Cor. 7:1 / Zephaniah 3:17 / Zechariah 2:5

---

[1] This is the "Seventh Day" of *My King.*

He is "the wall of fire round about," and "the glory in the midst of her"; and "he that toucheth you toucheth the apple of His eye." 3. *Joy.* Yes! "Be glad and rejoice with all the heart," "sing and rejoice, O daughter of Zion; for, lo, I come, and I will dwell in the midst of thee, saith the Lord."

Zechariah 2:8
Zephaniah 3:14
Zechariah 2:10

---

[1]FULL SATISFACTION IN THE KING.

"Yea, let him take all, forasmuch as my lord the king is come again in peace to his own house."—2 SAMUEL 19:30.

It is when the King has really come in peace to His own home in the "contrite and humble spirit" (not before),—when He has entered in to make His abode there (not before),—that the soul is satisfied with Him alone, and is ready to let any Ziba take all else, because all else really seems nothing at all in comparison to the conscious possession of the Treasure of treasures.

Isaiah 57:15
John 14:23
Psalm 22:26

Matthew 13:46

Sometimes this is reached at once, in the first flush of wondering joy at finding the King really "come in peace" to the empty soul which wanted to be "His own house." Sometimes very gradually, as year after year we realize His indwelling more and more, and find again and again that He is quite enough to satisfy us in all circumstances; that the empty corners of the "house" are filled one after another; that the old longings have somehow gone away, and the old ambitions vanished; that the old tastes and interests in the things of the world are superseded by stronger tastes and interests in the things of Christ; that He is day by day more really *filling* our lives,—we "count" (because we really find) one thing after another "but loss for the excellency of the knowledge of Christ Jesus my Lord," till He leads us on to the rapturous joy of the "Yea, doubtless," and "*all* things!"

Isaiah 33:6
Hebrews 3:6

Psalm 4:6
Cf. Eccles. &
Song.

Ephesians 1:23
Philippians 3:8

Now, have we got as far as saying "*some* things," without being quite sure about "*all* things"? Do you see that it all hinges upon Jesus coming into the heart as "His *own* house,"—*altogether* "His own"? For if there are some rooms of which we do not give up the key,—some little sitting-room which we would like to keep as a little mental retreat, with a view from the window, which we do not quite want to give up,—some lodger whom we would rather not send away just yet,—some little dark closet which we have not resolution to open and set to rights,—of course the King has not full possession; it is not all and really "His own"; and the very misgiving about it proves that

Acts 26:29

---

[1] This is the "Eighth Day" of *My King.*

He has *therefore* not yet "come again in peace." It is no use   Isaiah 26:3
expecting "perfect peace," while He has a secret controversy   Micah 6:2
with us about any withholding of what is "His own" by   Acts 5:2
purchase. Only throw open *all* the doors, "and the King of   Revelation 3:20
Glory shall come in," and then there will be no craving for   Psalm 24:9
other guests. He will "fill this house with glory," and there   Haggai 2:7
will be no place left for gloom.

    Is it not so? Bear witness, tell it out, you with whom
the King dwells in peace! Life is filled with bright interests,
time is filled with happy work or peaceful waiting, the mind
is filled with His beautiful words and thoughts, the heart   Proverbs 19:23
is filled with His presence, and you "abide satisfied" with
Him! Yes, "tell it out!"

The human heart asks love; but now I know
That my heart hath from Thee
All real, and full, and marvellous affection,
So near, so human! yet Divine perfection
Thrills gloriously the mighty glow!
Thy love is enough for me!

There were strange soul-depths, restless, vast and broad,
Unfathomed as the sea;
An infinite craving for some infinite stilling;
But now Thy perfect love is perfect filling!
Lord Jesus Christ, my Lord, my God,
Thou, Thou art enough for me.

[1]PREFATORY NOTE

"A Royal Commandment from Him!" Some of His Royal Commandments
are made so "plain upon tables, that he may run that readeth." Some are
carved between the lines of the tablets of sacred history, and flash out only as
the candle of the Lord falls upon them. Some are engraved upon the gems of
promise; and as we look closely into the fair colours of each jewel that the hand
of faith receives, we find that it is enriched by an unerasable line of precept. But
all are royal, for all are "from Him," our King. And He has said, "If ye love
Me, keep My commandments."

    The aim of this little book is to lead His servants, morning by morning, not
only to keep, but to seek, recognise, and delight in His Royal Commandments,
and it is sent forth with the prayer that every reader may be taught by His good
Spirit more of the happy "obedience of faith."

    It is hoped that the little companion volume, *Royal Bounty, or Evening
Thoughts for the King's Guests*, may be a tiny "cup of cold water" to some of
His tired children when their day's work, or day's waiting, is over. Both are

---

[1] This "Prefatory Note" was written at the front of *Royal Commandments*, which was published
together with *Royal Bounty* in 1877.

offered, very gratefully and lovingly, to the readers of *My King* who have spread those simple "Daily Thoughts" so far beyond the writer's expectation, with the earnest request that they will join in thanksgiving for the blessing which *has* been given, and in prayer that even greater blessing may be sent with these little books, for our Lord Jesus Christ's sake.

---

[1]THE ROYAL BOUNTY.

"And King Solomon gave unto the queen of Sheba all her desire, whatsoever she asked, beside that which Solomon gave her of his royal bounty."—1 KINGS 10:13.

ALL God's goodness to us is humbling. The more He does for us, the more ready we are to say, "I am not worthy of the least of all the mercies, and of all the truth, which Thou hast shewed unto Thy servant." The weight of a great answer to prayer seems almost too much for us. The grace of it is "too wonderful" for us. It throws up in such startling relief the disproportion between our little, poor, feeble cry, and the great shining response of God's heart and hand, that we can only say: "Who am I, O Lord God, that Thou hast brought me hitherto? Is this the manner of man, O Lord God?" — Genesis 32:10 / Luke 5:8, 9 / Job 42:3 / 2 Samuel 7:18–19

But it is more humbling still, when we stand face to face with great things which the Lord hath done for us and given us, which we never asked at all, never even thought of asking—royal bounty, with which not even a prayer had to do. It is so humbling to get a view of these, that Satan tries to set up a false humility to hinder us from standing still and considering how great things the Lord hath done for us; thus he also contrives to defraud our generous God of the glory due unto His name. — Psalm 126:3 / 1 Kings 3:13 / 1 Samuel 12:7, 24 / Psalm 29:2

For, of course, we do not praise for what we will not recognise.

Let us try to baffle this device to-day, and give thanks for the overwhelming mercies for which we never asked. "Blessed be the Lord, who daily loadeth us with benefits." Just think of them deliberately (they are far too many to think of all in a flash); and how many did we actually ask for? Even that poor little claim was never brought to bear on thousands of them. — Isaiah 63:7 / Psalm 68:19 / Psalm 103:2

To begin at the beginning, we certainly did not ask Him to choose us in Christ Jesus before the world began, and to predestinate us to be conformed to the image of His Son. Was not that "royal bounty" indeed? — 2 Thess. 2:13 / Ephesians 1:4 / Romans 8:29

---

[1] This is the "First Day" of the 31-day book *Royal Bounty*.

Then, we certainly did not ask Him to call us by His grace; for before that call we could not have wished, much less asked, for it. Then, who taught us to pray, and put into our entirely corrupt and sinful hearts any thought of asking Him for anything at all? Was not all this "royal bounty?" *2 Timothy 1:9; Romans 1:6 Luke 11:1 Job 37:19 Romans 8:26*

Look back at our early prayers. Has He not more than granted them? did we even know how much He could do for us? did He not answer prayer by opening out new vistas of prayer before us, giving us grace to ask for more grace, faith to plead for more faith? Why, it is *all* "royal bounty" from beginning to end! And this is going on now, and will go on for ever, when He has brought us with gladness and rejoicing into His own palace. Not till then shall we understand about those riches of glory in Christ Jesus, out of which He is even now pouring out the supply of all our need. *John 1:16; Romans 1:17; Luke 17:5 Psalm 45:15 Philippians 4:19*

The marginal reading is very beautiful; it is, "that which he gave her *according to the hand* of King Solomon." We may link this with David's grateful words: "*According to Thine own heart* hast Thou done all these great things"; and again: "Thou hast dealt well with Thy servant, O Lord, *according to Thy word*." His hand, His heart, His word— what an immeasurable measure of His bounty! The great *hand* that holds the ocean in its hollow is opened to satisfy our desire, and to go beyond that exceeding abundantly, giving us according to the *heart* that "*so* loved the world," and according to the *word* which is so deep and full that all the saints that ever drew their hope and joy from it cannot fathom its ever up-springing fountain. *2 Samuel 7:21 Psalm 119:65 Isaiah 40:12 Psalm 145:16 Ephesians 3:20 John 3:16 John 4:11, 14*

Perhaps nobody knows the Bible well enough to know the full significance of saying, "Be it unto me *according to Thy word*," how much less can we imagine what shall be the yet unrevealed royal bounty *according to His heart* of infinite love and hand of infinite power! "What I do thou knowest not now, but thou shalt know hereafter." "And ye shall … be satisfied, and praise the name of the Lord your God, that hath dealt wondrously with you." *Luke 1:38 John 13:7 Joel 2:26*

> When this passing world is done,
> When has sunk yon glaring sun,
> When we stand with Christ in glory,
> Looking o'er life's finished story,
> Then, Lord, shall I fully know—
> Not till then—how much I owe!
>
> R. M'CHEYNE.

[1]THE BRIGHT SIDE OF GROWING OLDER.

"And thine age shall be clearer than the noonday; thou shalt shine forth, thou shalt be as the morning."—JOB 11:17.

I suppose nobody ever did naturally like the idea of getting older, after they had at least "left school." There is a sense of oppression and depression about it. The irresistible, inevitable onward march of moments and years without the possibility of one instant's pause—a march that, even while on the uphill side of life, is leading to the downhill side—casts an autumn-like shadow over even many a spring birthday; for perhaps this is never more vividly felt than when one is only passing from May to June,—sometimes earlier still. But how surely the Bible gives us the bright side of everything! In this case it gives three bright sides of a fact, which, without it, could not help being gloomy.

> Eccles. 1:4, 5
> Eccles. 11:8
> Job 9:25
> Psalm 90:9, 10

First, it opens the sure prospect of *increasing brightness* to those who have begun to walk in the light. Even if the sun of our life has reached the apparent zenith, and we have known a very noonday of mental and spiritual being, it is no poetic "western shadows" that are to lengthen upon our way, but "our age is to be *clearer* than the noonday." How suggestive that word is! The light, though intenser and nearer, shall dazzle less; "in Thy light shall we *see* light," be able to bear much more of it, see it more clearly, see all else by it more clearly, reflect it more clearly. We should have said, "At evening-time there shall be shadow"; God says, "At evening-time there shall be light."

> 1 John 1:7
> Job 11:17
> Psalm 36:9
> Zechariah 14:7

Also, we are not to look for a very dismal afternoon of life with only some final sunset glow; for He says it "shineth more and more unto the perfect day"; and "more and more" leaves no dark intervals; we are to expect a continually brightening path. "The future is one vista of brightness and blessedness" to those who are willing only to "walk in the light." Just think, when you are seven, or ten, or twenty years older, that will only mean seven, or ten, or twenty years" more experience of His love and faithfulness, more light of the knowledge of the glory of God in the face of Jesus Christ; and *still* the "more and more unto the *perfect* day," will be opening out before us! We are "confident of this very thing!"

> Proverbs 4:18
> John 8:12
> 1 John 1:7
> 2 Cor. 4:6
> Proverbs 4:18
> Philippians 1:6

The second bright side is *increasing fruitfulness*. Do not let us confuse between works and fruit. Many a saint in the land of Beulah is not able to *do* anything at all, and yet is bringing forth fruit unto God beyond the busiest workers.

> Matthew 7:20, 22
> Romans 7:4

---

[1] This is the "Twenty-eighth Day" of *Royal Bounty*.

So that even when we come to the days when "the strong men shall bow themselves," there may be more pleasant fruits for our Master, riper and fuller and sweeter, than ever before. For "they shall still bring forth fruit in old age"; and the man that simply "trusteth in the Lord" "shall not be careful in the year of drought, neither shall cease from yielding fruit."

Eccles. 12:3
Song. 7:13; 4:16
Psalm 92:14
Jeremiah 17:7, 8

Some of the fruits of the Spirit seem to be especially and peculiarly characteristic of sanctified older years; and do we not want to bring them *all* forth? Look at the splendid ripeness of Abraham's "faith" in his old age; the grandeur of Moses' "meekness," when he went up the mountain alone to die; the mellowness of St. Paul's "joy" in his later epistles; and the wonderful "gentleness" of St. John, which makes us almost forget his early character of "a son of thunder," wanting to call down God's lightnings of wrath. And "the same Spirit" is given to us, that we too may bring forth "fruit that may abound," and always "more fruit."

Galatians 5:22, 23
Romans 4:19–21
Deut. 34:1, 5
Ephesians and
Philippians
Mark 3:17
Luke 9:54
1 Cor. 12:13
Phil 4:17; Jn 15:2

The third bright side is brightest of all: *"Even to your old age, I am He"*; always the same Jehovah-Jesus; with us "all the days," bearing and carrying us "all the days"; reiterating His promise—"even to hoar hairs will I carry you … ; even I will carry and will deliver you," just as He carried the lambs in His bosom. For we shall always be His little children, and "doubtless" He will always be our Father. The rush of years cannot touch this!

Isaiah 46:4
Matthew 28:20
Isaiah 63:9
Isaiah 46:4
Isaiah 40:11
1 John 2:13
Isaiah 63:16
Hebrews 1:11, 12

> Fear not the westering shadows,
>   O Children of the Day!
> For brighter still and brighter,
>   Shall be your homeward way.
> Resplendent as the morning,
>   With fuller glow and power,
> And clearer than the noonday,
>   Shall be your evening hour.

---

[1]OUR SWISS GUIDE

Not the least interesting part of mountaineering is the perpetual upspringing of lessons and illustrations and analogies. Sometimes an idea starts up which has, for one's self, all the delicious charm of a quite new thought, though very likely it may have flashed upon the minds of scores of other travellers; sometimes a

[1] "Our Swiss Guide" was first published in the periodical *Sunday Magazine* in 1874, and was later published in the posthumous *Swiss Letters and Alpine Poems* edited by her eldest sister Miriam (London: James Nisbet & Co., 1881), pages 304-318. This article can be found on pages 353-356 of Volume IV of Havergal's *Complete Works*. F.R.H. was utterly fluent in German and French (and nearly fluent in Italian).

very old and familiar one presents itself, and we have the pleasure of proving it, perhaps for the first time, by practical experience. In noting one little group of illustrations among many, those which cluster round the idea of a "Guide," we shall not be careful to steer clear of such old ideas, though we may hope to add some freshness to them.

The application throughout will be so very obvious to any mind accustomed to take the least interest in analogies of spiritual life, that we prefer giving the points of illustration only, leaving the reader to supply the "heavenly meaning" which shall underlie each sentence.

Curiously enough, the name of our favourite Swiss guide, the one who inspired us with most confidence, and to whom we should most like to entrust ourselves in any future tour, at once gave the keynote of thought; it was *Joseph.* While we instinctively trusted his sagacity and strength, it was additionally pleasant to find that our bright young guide was a believer in the Lord Jesus Christ, our true Joseph. He had remarked that his great physical strength and health was "the most splendid earthly gift," but on our mention of the most glorious Gift of all, our Saviour Christ himself, he rejoined fervently, "Ah, one can never estimate the value of *that* gift!"

But to proceed to our illustrations.

1. The first duty of a really firstrate guide, when arranging for a long snow or glacier excursion, is to see that we are properly provided with everything needful. He ascertains that you have snow spectacles, without which the glare of the snow is not simply inconvenient, but injurious; and veils, without which you stand a fair chance of finding your face completely flayed, if it should be a sunny day. He examines the spike of your alpenstock and the nails of your boots, and inquires after your wraps, and often gives curiously practical advice as to other points in your outfit. He not only tells you what you must have as to provision, but, if the excursion involves a night in some mountain hut, he sends on the necessary fuel and food, and sometimes even bedding. In all these matters you do not need to trouble at all; if you will only leave it altogether to him, he will think of everything, arrange everything, and provide everything; and when the time comes you will find all in order, your shoes fresh nailed, your alpenstock newly spiked, the porter sent on with provision, and the coil of strong rope and the ice axe all ready for the difficult places which you do not yet know of.

But many travellers do not even know that the guide is thus willing and competent; they do not ask, or perhaps they even decline, his aid and advice. Instead of throwing it all upon his responsibility, they take all the trouble themselves, and then generally find something gone wrong or something overlooked.

2. Before you start, the guide has disposed of all those heavier matters which you could not possibly carry for yourself. Very often they are taken completely out of your sight. Encumbered with these, you could not even set out on your

journey, much less progress quickly and pleasantly.

But there are always plenty of little affairs which seem mere nothings at first, but which are soon found to be real burdens. The guide is perfectly willing to relieve you of all these. They are no weight to him; he quite smiles at the idea of its being any trouble to him to carry them, but they make a serious difference to you. He offers to take them at first; and if you decline, though he may not perhaps offer again, he will cheerfully take them when, later on, you feel their weight, and hand them one by one to him, till the very last is given up, and you walk lightly and freely. A beginner says she "would rather carry her little knapsack, it is really no weight at all!" and thinks a parcel or two in her pocket "can't make any difference," and prefers wearing her waterproof, because "it isn't at all heavy." But she has not gone far before she is very glad, if a sensible girl, to give up her knapsack, tiny though it be; and then she finds that a waterproof won't do for climbing, and she hands that over; and presently she even empties her pocket, and the guide trudges away with it all. Then she is surprised to find what a difference it does make, and understands why her friend, who knew the guide's ways better and gave up every single thing to him at first, is getting along so cool and fresh and elastically. But mark that the weight of a burden is seldom realized till we really are going uphill and in a fair way to make progress. Indeed, this very sensitiveness to weight is a quick test of increased gradient. We think nothing about it as long as we are walking on a level or slightly downhill; but as soon as we begin the real ascent the pull of the little burdens is felt at once, and the assistance, which before we did not crave, becomes very welcome. It is then that we feel we *must* "lay aside *every* weight."

3. One may almost certainly distinguish between a tyro and an old hand by watching for a few minutes the style of march. A novice will walk at an irregular pace according to the irregularities of the ground, making little "spurts" when she comes to an easy bit, and either putting on steam or lagging behind for extra steep ones; stopping to gather flowers and poke at curious boulders; taking long or short steps according to circumstances, and never thinking of such a thing as noticing, much less imitating, the steady rhythm of the guide's walk. Probably she expresses her astonishment at his unexpectedly slow pace, and would prefer getting on a little faster; very likely she dashes ahead or aside, and presently has to be recalled to the track, which is not so easy to keep as she supposed.

One with more experience is quite content to take the guide's pace, knowing certainly that it pays in the long run, and saves an enormous amount of fatigue, and therefore of time also. Very short steps, slowly, silently, and steadily placed, but as regular as martial music, never varying in beat, never broken by alternation of strides and pauses—this is the guide's example for uphill work; and yet it is what one never believes in till one has learnt by experience that one gets through twice as much by it.

4. It is wonderful what a saving of fatigue it is if from the very beginning one obeys the guide implicitly and follows him exactly. You spy such a handy "short cut," you can see so precisely where you can join the path again, it will

save you such a provoking long round, you can't think why the guide does not choose it! So away you go, exulting in your cleverness, straight uphill, instead of that tiresome zigzag.

But it is rather steeper than you thought, and you get just a little out of breath; and you find an awkward little perpendicular rock right in the way and you must go round it; and then you get into rhododendron bushes which are thicker than you thought, and you get very wet; and then you see your companions reaching the point you are making for, and you scramble and hurry. And by the time you have done with your short cut you find you have not only gained no time, but that the few minutes away from the guide have heated you and taken more out of you than an hour's steady following. Later in the day you recollect your short cuts of the morning, and wish you had economised your breath.

5. The full value of exact following is not learnt in the valleys or pastures. It is on the "high places" and on the unsullied snowfields that one discovers this.

It is when we are high away above the green slopes, seeing no track but our guide's own footsteps, that we learn its safety. He set his foot on that stone: there you must set yours, for the next is loose and would betray you; he planted his alpenstock on that inch of rock: there you must plant yours, for an inch either way would give no firm hold; he climbed by that jut of rock: so must you, for the other would be too hard a step; he sprang but half way over that torrent, and you must do the same at cost of wetting your feet, for he knew that the slab of rock which you could have reached at one bound was treacherously slippery and dangerous.

It is here also that we get into the way of instant and unquestioning compliance with every word our guide utters. I was struck with the remark of a Swiss Alpine Clubbist in a description of his ascent of the Tödi. His guide suddenly shouted to him, "Turn sharp to the right!" He saw no reason whatever for this, but obeyed instantly. The next moment an immense block of stone fell upon the spot where he would have been had he hesitated an instant or even looked round to satisfy himself. The quick and practised eye of the guide saw the trembling of the loosened mass which the traveller could not see. A query would have been fatal. He added, "In these high places one learns to obey one's guide without stopping to ask 'Why?'"

But when the snow slopes, so cool and pure and beautiful, are reached, another phase of following is learnt. There is not the excitement and effort of the rock climbing, and at first it seems very quiet and easy work, with a special exhilaration of its own, making one feel as if one had started quite fresh, all the rest of the journey counting for nothing. Once we set out on such a slope, tracking after our guide in a general sort of way, rather interested in making our own footprints, and hardly distinguishing his from those of our companions. If we turned to look back, it was surprising what a number of unconscious little curves our feet had made. But the snow was rather soft, and we soon found it much harder work than we expected. One of us was walking, as she always did, close behind the guide, because she was not quite so strong as the rest, and was therefore under his especial care. Suddenly she called out, "Oh, do set your feet *exactly* in the guide's footsteps, you can't think how much easier it is!" So we tried it, and certainly should not have believed what a difference it would make. All the difficulty and effort seemed gone; the fatiguing sinking and laborious lifting of our feet were needless; we set them now exactly where the guide's great foot had trodden, keeping his order of right and left, and all was easy, a hundred steps less toil than twenty before. But, to have the full benefit of this, one needed to keep also very near to the guide, for the last comers trod rather in their companions' footmarks, and were often misled by some false or uncertain treading of these, which marred the perfectness of the original steps.

6. Thorough knowledge of the guide's language adds both to the enjoyment and safety of our following. He has much to tell us by the way, and is always ready to answer questions and give information. One who does not easily understand loses a great deal. A companion may be very willing to translate, but may do so incorrectly, and in any case the freshness and point of many a remark is lost; while it often happens that the usual interpreter of a party is not near enough for appeal or too tired to keep up the interchange. In sudden emergencies too it may be really important that each should personally understand, and thus be able instantly to obey, the guide's directions.

Moreover, it is very desirable not only thus to "know his voice," but to be able to speak to him for one's self. Once one of us slipped in a rather awkward place. She called out, "Stop a moment!" but the guide in advance knew no English, and therefore did not heed her, and but for the quick call in German of another who saw the slip, she might have been frightened and hurt.

7. When we come to really difficult places, or glaciers with hidden crevasses, we find the use of the coil of rope. This is fastened first round the guide himself, and then round the rest of the party, allowing a length of eight or ten feet between each. Once I questioned the strength of the rope, upon which the guide untwisted it a little, and showed me a scarlet thread hidden among the strands. He told me that this was the mark that it was a real Alpine Club rope, manufactured expressly for the purpose, and to be depended upon in a matter of life and death. It is remarkable that this typical "line of scarlet thread" should have been selected as the guarantee of safety.

Once roped thus, you have a sense of security in passing what would otherwise be very dangerous places, especially concealed crevasses. And not only a sense but a reality of security. You feel the snow yield beneath your feet, you sink in, and you have neither hand nor foothold; you get perhaps a glimpse of a fathomless blue depth below you. If you struggle you only break away the snow and enlarge the cavity. But you are in no real danger, and if you have confidence in your guide and the rope, you wait quietly, perhaps even smilingly, till you are hauled out of the hole, and landed on firm snow again. Why? Because you are firmly knotted to your guide, and also to all the rest of your party. You had not even time to call out ere he felt the sudden strain upon the rope, and instantly turned to help you, drawing you easily up to his side without hurt. Your friends felt the shock too but they could not do much to help, only they watched and admired the guide, and found their own fears (if they had any) lessened, and their confidence in him and his rope greatly increased.

But it is the guide himself who bears the brunt of these difficulties. He goes first, carefully sounding the snow, avoiding many a crevasse which we should never have suspected, and sometimes getting a fall which would have been ours but for his trying the way for us. If we really follow his steps exactly and patiently, the probability is that we never go in at all, for the snow that has borne his weight never gives way under ours. But if we swerve even a few inches from his footmarks, we may soon find ourselves in the predicament described above.

8. Sometimes we come to a slope of frozen snow so steep that it looks absolutely impossible to climb it. And so it would be, but for our guide. Our impossibilities only develop his resources. Now he unshoulders his ice axe, and with wonderful rapidity cuts steps by which we ascend even more easily than hitherto. And we notice that these extra-difficult slopes are a positive advantage to us, because while he has all the hard work we have time to take breath. When the steep bit is passed, we have gained greatly in height, and yet we feel quite freshened for further ascent, instead of fatigued.

9. The guide decides your rest as well as your progress, if you are wise enough to let him. He very soon measures your powers, and not only knows precisely when a crevasse is just too wide for you to leap without help, or a rock just too awkward for you to climb, but he also seems to know precisely when you had better make longer or shorter halts. Sometimes you are unwilling to rest when he proposes it, and perhaps he lets you have your own way and go on, and then you are quite certain to be sorry for it. But more often he insists, and then you always find he was right, and that he had timed the halt better than you would have done. Then, without waiting to be asked, he unfastens your wraps, contrives a seat upon the snow, and folds a shawl round you. It is no use saying you do not feel cold, he is responsible for you, and knows what is safe, and will not let you risk getting chilled by the subtle glacier wind. Then he gives you the provision he has carried for you, meat, and bread, and wine, and leaves no little stone unturned towards making your halt as refreshing and pleasant as possible. There is no need for you to be calculating time, and fidgeting about going on; he knows how much is yet before you, and he will tell you when it is time to be moving again.

10. I mentioned that the weakest of our party was specially cared for. Sometimes while the others had merely general orders, she had his strong arm, and thus escaped the slips which the more independent ones now and then made. Weakness or ailments proved his patience and care. On one occasion the "mountain sickness" which sometimes befalls travellers on great heights suddenly attacked one not accustomed to fail in strength, and then nothing could exceed Joseph's kindness and attention. He made a wonderfully comfortable couch on the snow, told us what was the matter, administered advice and wine, and waited patiently and sympathetically till his patient, completely prostrate for an hour, felt able to stand. Then in a firm decided tone he said, "*Ich* übernehme die Kranke!" (*I* undertake the sick one!) and leaving the other guides to attend to all else, his powerful arm helped "die Kranke" down to a level where the less rarefied air soon set all to rights.

11. It is understood that a true Swiss guide is literally "faithful unto death," that he does not hesitate to risk his own life for the sake of his charge, and that instances are known in which it has not only been risked but actually sacrificed. We have never been in a position to prove this, but the undoubted fact completes the illustration. Yet this completion only shows the imperfection. For that poor faithful guide may perish *with* the traveller, and not *instead* of him; the sacrifice may be all in vain where the power and the will are not commensurate. In such illustrations we may learn as much by the contrasts as by the similiarities; and how often, as in this instance, does the very failure of an earthly type bring out the glory and perfection of the Antitype. Our glorious Guide, who has called us to the journey, and whose provision for it is "without money and without price," cannot fail in His undertaking. All who are in His covenant hands are "kept by the power of God through faith unto salvation," and "shall never perish." What He hath begun He will perform, for He "is able to keep you from falling, and to present you faultless before the presence of His glory with exceeding joy." He is not merely willing to lay down His life, but He hath laid it down for us, and now death cannot touch our Leader any more; He hath "the power of an endless life," and we are united to that life by the strong cords of His eternal purpose and His everlasting love, which no friction can weaken and no stroke can sever. However tremendous the gulf beneath us, if thus united to Him, He will lead us on till our feet, no longer weary, stand far above the clouds upon the mountain of our God, never to repass the toils and dangers of the ascent, never to return to the valley, never to part from the strong and loving Guide who has led us to such a Hitherto of rest and wonder, and to such a Henceforth of joy and praise.

---

[1]I DO NOT FEAR DEATH

Extract from F. R. H.'s MS., in answer to a remark:
"Death, which we ALL dread."

No, not "All!" One who has seen and *accepted* God's way of salvation, does *not* dread death. Perhaps I shall best express myself by doing it very personally —just giving my own experience.

I do not fear death. Often I wake in the night and think of it, look forward to it, with a thrill of joyful expectation and anticipation, which would become impatience, were it not that Jesus is my Master, as well as my Saviour, and I feel I have work to do for Him that I would not shirk, and also that *His* time to call me home will be the *best* and *right* time; therefore I am content to wait.

---

[1] This piece, a clear, powerful presentation of the truth of salvation in Christ, was taken from a manuscript by F.R.H., published in Mrs. Stephen Menzies' valuable compilation *The Traveller's Guide from Death to Life* (London: S. W. Partridge & Co., no date, likely 1880-1900). This is found on pages 690-691 of Volume II of Havergal's *Complete Works.* Mrs. Menzies was a colleague of F.R.H. in the Young Women's Christian Association, and at least 200,000 copies of her book were printed, likely more.

One night I was conscious of certain symptoms preluding an all but fatal attack (of erysipelas) I had had once before on the brain.

I knew, if means failed, it was probably my last night on earth. I let my mother attend to me, but alarmed no one, and I was left alone in bed. Then, alone in the dark, I felt it might be my last conscious hour on earth, and that either sleep or fatal unconsciousness would set in. I never spent a calmer, sweeter hour than that. I had not one shadow of fear! only happy rest and confidence in Him "Whom I have believed."

Was this delusion? Could it be so in the very face of death, that great *un*masker of all uncertainties? I knew it was not delusion, for "I know Whom I have believed."

It was not always thus. I know as well as any one, what it is to "*dread death*," and to put away the thought of its absolute certainty, because I dare not look it in the face.

There was a time when I saw clearly I could *not* save myself—that I deserved hell in many ways, but in one most of all, this—that I owed the whole love of my heart to God, and had not given it to Him; that Jesus had *so* loved me as to *die for me,* and yet I had treated Him with daily, hourly ingratitude. I had broken the first commandment, and as I owed all my life—future and past—to God, I had literally "*nothing to pay*"; for living to Him, and keeping His commands for the future, would not atone for the past. I saw the sinfulness of my heart and life. I could not make my heart better. "*The soul that sinneth it shall die.*" So, unless sin *is* taken away, my soul *must die and go to hell.*

Where then was my hope? In the same Word of God (1 John 5:10), it is written, "He that believeth on the Son hath the witness in himself," and (John 3:36), "He that believeth on the Son *hath everlasting life:* and he that believeth *not* the Son shall not see life; but the *wrath* of God abideth on Him."

Believe what?—that He *must* keep His word and punish sin, and that He *has* punished it in the person of Jesus, *our Substitute,* "Who His own self bare our sins in His own body on the tree" (1 Peter 2:24).

If Jesus has paid *my* debt, and borne the punishment of *my* sins, I simply accept this, and believe Him, and it is all a true and real transaction. I did this—I believed it, and cast myself, utterly hopeless and helpless in myself, at the feet of Jesus, took Him at His word, and accepted what He had done for me.

Result?—Joy, peace in believing, and a happy, FULL trust in Him, which death cannot touch.

Now it is a reality of realities to me—it is so intertwined with my life, that I know nothing could separate me from His love.

I could not do without Jesus. I cannot and I do not live without Him. It is a *new* and different life; and the life and light which takes away *all fear of death,* is what I want others to have and enjoy.

"Death is swallowed up in *victory.* O death, where is thy sting? O grave, where is thy victory? The sting of death is sin; and the strength of sin is the law. But thanks be to God, which giveth us the victory through our Lord Jesus Christ" (1 Cor. 15:54-57).

[1]TO THE MEMBERS OF THE
YOUNG WOMEN'S CHRISTIAN ASSOCIATION.

"We believe, and therefore speak." 2 Corinthians 4:13.

DEAR sister-workers, may we, prayerfully depending on the Holy Spirit's teaching, find in these words a stimulus to greater faithfulness to our membership, greater effort for our Master.

WHAT *do we believe?* "The glorious Gospel of Christ." A true belief in this is no light thing. Could we sever it from our hearts, what would be left but a very death in life? However feeble, it is *precious* faith.

How *do we believe?* What is the practical result for others? We meet with those who have not "like precious faith," and we are content to speak only of what is nothing worth. Yet each is in the danger from which we have fled, each has the same soul-needs. If we believed that she with whom we are lightly exchanging pleasant or necessary remarks, must perish for ever unless Jesus saves her, should we not "therefore speak?" Let us try to realize. The young friend or stranger at my side, if she does not know Jesus, has no Friend, no Comforter, no share in all my happiness, nothing to fill an aching void within. But more:—This very one, if she does not know Jesus, must be shut out from Him for ever, and endure the unknown terrors of God's wrath for ever, and ever, and ever. There is but a step between her and death, and this may be her last opportunity to hear of the Saviour's love. Can I believe these truths, and part from her with smiling nothings, without one word to arouse, to win, to save?

WHAT *shall we speak?* Say that to God. He will give us words. With our highest skill, we can but draw the bow at a venture, for the mark is hidden. Let us trust in Him Who can and will both give and guide the arrow. An imperceptible pause in conversation is time enough for an unworded prayer, a heart-glance up to Him for the right words, and for those words to be flashed into our minds, in swift and gracious answer. Let our hearts be filled with Christ and His salvation, and out of their abundance our mouths will speak.

WHEN *shall we speak?* Conscience will tell us. It will tell us, too, that we do not want more opportunities so much as grace to see and to use those which are continually given. Which of us can count lost opportunities? Yet our Master noted each one as it passed. Let not the number be increased this year. It may be that a sense of coldness and sin is heavy upon us, and we hardly dare to speak of truths which have so little power over ourselves. Yet it does not say—"We *feel*, and therefore speak," but "We *believe*." Could we say that we do *not* believe? or quietly endure to hear our Saviour's name and work denied? Even in our suffering we may tell a fellow-sufferer of a cure; and while laying her case before the Great Physician, we shall find that He is nearer than we thought, and that His healing and reviving hand is laid upon ourselves. "The Lord turned the captivity of Job when he prayed for his friends." "He that watereth shall be watered."

---

[1] This "Open Letter" was a printed leaflet, found among Havergal's manuscripts and papers. This is found on pages 965-966 of Volume II of Havergal's *Complete Works*.

How *shall we speak?* One who has had long experience among Middle Eastern women lately said:—" If we would do them good, *we must love them.*" This is the secret of reaching English girls, as well as Syrian maidens; the feather that wings our arrow must be *love,* and if love be real, it will be seen and felt. It flows spontaneously to some, but how shall we command it for all whom we would reach? Only believe the word—" He died for all." Realize that Jesus so loved them that He died for them, and you will catch your Master's spirit, and speak with that winningness which love alone can give.

Let us make a second application of our motto, which yet must come first in practice. If we believe, let us therefore speak much *to* our God for every one to whom we would speak *of* Him. Does He anywhere set any limit to expectant prayer except His will? And "He willeth not the death of a sinner." What unknown blessings we may have lost by restraining prayer! What unknown blessings may be granted us, even this year, only for the asking! Will every one connected with the Association pray especially that God would pour " the spirit of grace and of supplication " upon every Branch and every Member through the coming year? Then how many prayers will be transmuted into praise! Let us look forward, not merely with hope, but expectation; believing that not we alone, and not the angels only, but our beloved Master Himself, will rejoice and be very glad over those for whom we pray. Sooner or later, we who "believe, and therefore speak," shall see, and therefore sing.

LORD, INCREASE OUR FAITH. LORD, OPEN THOU OUR LIPS.

IV. MUSIC

These six music scores by F.R.H. are found in these locations in the edition of Havergal's Complete Works: Volume V, entitled *Songs of Truth and Love: Music by Frances Ridley Havergal and William Henry Havergal,* has these scores in facsimile reprints of the original 19th century published scores. The Companion Volume to the edition, entitled Music by Frances Ridley Havergal, has these in newly typeset scores prepared by Dr. Glen T. Wegge.

In the Prefatory Note to the very valuable volume *Loyal Responses* with music, posthumously published, Frances' sister Maria gave this quotation of her:

> "I am delighted to have an opportunity of adding to the very meagre supply of Sacred Songs, and I hope they will be sufficiently tuneful and sufficiently easy for drawing-room singing. Some of those extant are very pathetic and dismal affairs! Why put off joyous singing till we reach the happier shore? Let us sing words which we feel and love, with clearness of enunciation, and looking up to meet His smile all the while we are singing. So shall we loyally sing for our King, yes for Him, Whose voice is our truest music." [F.R.H.]

HERMAS

Psalm 55:23. *"I will trust in Thee."*

Music by Frances Ridley Havergal
Words by Mary Jane Walker, 1864

6 5, 6 5, D.

Je - sus, I will trust Thee, trust Thee with my soul;

Guilt - y, lost, and help - less, Thou canst make me whole.

There is none in hea - ven or on earth like Thee:

Thou hast died for sin - ners — there-fore, Lord, for me. A - men.

2. Jesus, I may trust Thee, name of
    matchless worth
  Spoken by the angel at Thy
    wondrous birth;
  Written, and for ever, on Thy
    cross of shame,
  Sinners read and worship,
    trusting in that name.

3. Jesus, I must trust Thee,
    pondering Thy ways,
  Full of love and mercy all Thine
    earthly days:
  Sinners gathered round Thee,
    lepers sought Thy face—
  None too vile or loathsome for a
    Saviour's grace.

4. Jesus, I can trust Thee, trust Thy
    written word,
  Though Thy voice of pity I have
    never heard.
  When Thy Spirit teacheth, to my
    taste how sweet—
  Only may I hearken, sitting at
    Thy feet.

5. Jesus, I do trust Thee, trust
    without a doubt:
  "Whosoever cometh, Thou wilt
    not cast out."
  Faithful is Thy promise, precious
    is Thy blood—
  These my soul's salvation, Thou
    my Saviour God !

LOVE FOR LOVE.

Words and Music by
Frances Ridley Havergal

2. Knowing Christ was crucified,
　　Knowing that He loves you now
Just as much as when He died
　　With the thorns upon His brow,—
　　Stay and think !—
How He loves ! oh, should not you
Love this blessèd Saviour too ?

3. Knowing that a Spirit strives
　　With your weary, wandering heart,
Who can change the restless lives,
　　Pure and perfect peace impart,—
　　Stay and think !—
How He loves ! oh, should not you
Love this loving Spirit too ?

"NOW."

Five sailors were clinging to the broken mast of a sinking ship in Dublin Bay. A rope was thrown to them. At the trumpet signal "Now!" they were to loose their hold of the mast, and trust themsleves to the rope. Four did so, and were hauled safe to shore. The fifth hesitated to let go, and was lost!

Words and Music by
Frances Ridley Havergal

1.God's "Now" is sound ing in your ears, O let it reach your heart! From ev-'ry trust but Christ a-lone He bids you part. There

Chorus (to be sung after each verse)

is one hope, and on-ly one! You can be sav'd, but how? The rope hold fast, but quit the mast At the trum-pet sig-nal, "NOW!"

Your righteousness as filthy rags Must all relinquished be, And only Jesu's precious death Must be your plea.	Trust now the one provided rope, Quit now the broken mast ! Before the hope of safety be For ever past.	Fear not to trust His simple word, So sweet, so tried, so true ! And you are safe for evermore, Yes, even you !

TRUSTING JESUS.

Tune-Urbane II

Words and Music by
Frances Ridley Havergal

1.I am trust-ing Thee, Lord, Je-sus, Trust-ing on - ly Thee;

Trust-ing Thee for full sal-va-tion, Great and free.

2. I am trusting Thee for pardon;
   At Thy feet I bow,
For Thy grace and tender mercy,
   Trusting now.

3. I am trusting Thee for cleansing
   In the crimson flood;
Trusting Thee to make me holy
   By Thy blood.

4. I am trusting Thee to guide me;
   Thou alone shalt lead !
Every day and hour supplying
   All my need.

5. I am trusting Thee for power;
   Thine can never fail !
Words which Thou Thyself shalt give me,
   Must prevail.

6. I am trusting Thee, Lord Jesus;
   Never let me fall !
I am trusting Thee for ever,
   And for all.

ONLY FOR THEE.

Tune-Onesimus
Smoothly & Cheerfully

Music by Frances Ridley Havergal
Words by E. A. Walker

1.Pre - cious Sa - viour, may I live, On - ly for Thee!
2.Be my smiles and be my tears, On - ly for Thee!

Spend the pow - ers Thou dost give, On - ly for Thee!
Be my young and ri - per years, On - ly for Thee!

Be my spi - rit's deep de - sire, On - ly for
Be my peace and be my strife, On - ly for

THE LORD HATH DONE IT.

Words and Music by
Frances Ridley Havergal

2. I know that what He doeth
   Stands for ever, fixed and true;
   Nothing can be added to it,
   Nothing left for us to do.

Nothing can be taken from it.
Done for me, and done for you
Evermore and evermore.

3. Listen now! the Lord hath done it!
   For He loved us unto death;
   It is finished, He hath saved us!
   Only trust to what He saith!
   He hath done it, come and bless Him.
   Spend in praise your ransomed breath,
   Evermore and evermore.

4. O believe the Lord hath done it!
   Wherefore linger, wherefore doubt?
   All the cloud of black transgression
   He Himself hath blotted out.
   He hath done it, come and bless Him,
   Swell the grand thanksgiving shout
   Evermore and evermore.

"to fill up the leaf withal"

F.R.H. wrote in a letter in 1869, "I hope you will get to know Charlotte Elliott; it is an honour from God to have had it given her, to write what she has written."

THE PILGRIM'S WANT.

by Charlotte Elliott.

I want that adorning Divine,
Thou only, my God, canst bestow;
I want in those beautiful garments to shine,
Which distinguish Thy household below.
Colossians 3:12, 17

I want every moment to feel
That Thy Spirit resides in my heart,
That His power is present to cleanse and to heal,
And newness of life to impart.
Romans 8:11, 16

I want, oh! I want to attain
Some likeness, my Saviour, to Thee!
That longed-for resemblance once more to regain,
Thy comeliness put upon me!
1 John 3:2, 3

I want to be marked for Thine own,
Thy seal on my forehead to wear;
To receive that "new name" on the mystic white
Which none but Thyself can declare. [stone,
Revelation 2:17

I want so in Thee to abide,
As to bring forth some fruit to Thy praise!
The branch which Thou prunest, though feeble
May languish, but never decays. [and dried,
John 15:2, 5

I want Thine own hand to unbind
Each tie to terrestrial things—
Too tenderly cherished, too closely entwined,
Where my heart too tenaciously clings.
1 John 2:15

I want, by my aspect serene,
My actions and words to declare—
That my treasure is placed in a country unseen,
That my heart's best affections are there.
Matthew 6:19, 21

I want, as a traveller, to haste
Straight onward, nor pause in my way—
Nor forethought, nor anxious contrivance, to
On the tent only pitched for a day. [waste
Hebrews 13:5, 6

I want—and this sums up my prayer—
To glorify Thee till I die;
Then calmly to yield up my soul to Thy care,
And breathe out, in faith, my last sigh.
Philippians 3:8,9

ANNOUNCING THE HAVERGAL EDITION
NOW IN PREPARATION FOR PUBLICATION

The edition of *The Complete Works of Frances Ridley Havergal* has five parts:

Volume I *Behold Your King:*
  The Complete Poetical Works of Frances Ridley Havergal

Volume II *Whose I Am and Whom I Serve:*
  Prose Works of Frances Ridley Havergal

Volume III *Loving Messages for the Little Ones:*
  Works for Children by Frances Ridley Havergal

Volume IV *Love for Love:*
  Frances Ridley Havergal: Memorials, Letters and Biographical Works

Volume V *Songs of Truth and Love:*
  Music by Frances Ridley Havergal and William Henry Havergal

David L. Chalkley, Editor Dr. Glen T. Wegge, Music Editor

THE MUSIC OF FRANCES RIDLEY HAVERGAL
BY GLEN T. WEGGE, PH.D.

This Companion Volume to the Havergal edition is a valuable presentation of most or nearly all of F.R.H.'s extant scores. Very few of them, if any at all, have been much seen or often even known of for nearly a century. What a valuable body of music has been unknown for so long and is now made available to many! Dr. Wegge completed his Ph.D. in Music Theory at Indiana University at Bloomington, and his diligence and thoroughness in this volume are obvious. First an analysis of F.R.H.'s compositions is given, an essay that both addresses the most advanced musicians and also reaches those who are untrained in music; then all the extant scores that have been found are newly typeset, with complete texts for each score and extensive indices at the end of the book. This volume presents F.R.H.'s music in newly typeset scores diligently prepared by Dr. Wegge, and Volume V of the Havergal edition presents the scores in facsimile, the original 19th century scores. (The essay—a dissertation—analysing her scores is given the same both in this Companion Volume and in Volume V of the Havergal edition.)

  Dr. Wegge is also preparing all of these scores for publication in performance folio editions.

Frances Ridley Havergal Trust 4214 Wildrose Court
A Division of Granted Ministries Hannibal, Missouri 63401